ROYAL OAK BURIAL PARK
A History and Guide

"The modern burial park is not an aggregation of graves, but a place of rest and consolation for the sorrowing and bereaved. It is a place fit for deep, earnest thought: for profitable meditation and for devout worship. It brings comfort and joy to the wounded in heart and lifts the soul to higher planes. It reconciles the mind to death and speaks of life beyond the veil."

C. Hiram Babcock, 1922

DAVE OBEE

Published by Dave Obee, 4687 Falaise Drive, Victoria, B.C. V8Y 1B4 Canada.

Printed in Canada by Friesens.

Edited by Sarah Obee.

Front cover photographs:
• Royal Oak Burial Park, October 2007. By Dave Obee.
• Funeral of Thomas Hastings, August 1927. Image 1995-005-011 courtesy Saanich Archives.
Back cover photograph:
• Section B and the Garden Chapel, 1948. From Royal Oak Burial Park files.

Library and Archives Canada Cataloguing in Publication

Obee, Dave, 1953-
      Royal Oak Burial Park : a history and guide / Dave Obee.

Includes index.
ISBN 978-0-9735143-2-2

      1. Royal Oak Burial Park (Saanich, B.C.)--History. 2. Royal Oak
Burial Park (Saanich, B.C.)--Guidebooks. 3. Saanich (B.C.)--Biography.
I. Title.

FC3849.S218Z63 2008   971.1'28   C2008-900419-1

Royal Oak Burial Park

Royal Oak Burial Park is the largest municipal cemetery in British Columbia. It is a park filled with trees, flowers and lawns – a natural oasis in an increasingly urbanized corner of Vancouver Island. It was opened in 1923 as a replacement for Ross Bay Cemetery, which had been in operation on Victoria's waterfront for half a century.

Royal Oak is the final resting place for tens of thousands of people, including five premiers, other provincial, federal and municipal politicians, hockey stars, business leaders and entertainers.

This book is the culmination of more than 10 years of research. The project had its roots in simple strolls through the cemetery. It grew into a book with the realization that the burial park has a rich history, and has become the permanent home to many interesting people.

This is the first history and guide to Royal Oak Burial Park. It was compiled from a wide variety of sources, including minute books of the Board of Cemetery Trustees of Greater Victoria; back issues of the Times Colonist and its predecessors, the Daily Colonist and the Victoria Daily Times; and the air photography collection at the University of Victoria.

This book is not designed as a comprehensive account of everyone buried in or cremated at Royal Oak; that would require information on almost 150,000 people. It does, however, include brief biographies of many people who were interred in or cremated at the burial park. The biography section is selective, by necessity, although an attempt has been made to include a broad cross-section.

Sources consulted for the biography section include the Times, the Colonist and newspapers from other cities, the vital statistics records at the British Columbia Archives, files in the Saanich and Victoria municipal archives, and databases compiled by the Victoria Genealogical Society.

This work would not have been possible without the help of Stephen Olson, the executive director of Royal Oak Burial Park. Others who provided valuable assistance include burial park employees such as Ray Laursen and Brian Nickels; Ben Elwell, whose family once owned part of the cemetery land; local resident Franca LaBella; Saanich Chief Constable Derek Egan; Michael Carter of the B.C. Archives; and Caroline Duncan of the Saanich municipal archives.

Unless otherwise noted, photographs are from the files at Royal Oak Burial Park or were taken by the author.

We hope this history and guide will encourage more people to visit Royal Oak Burial Park, and come to appreciate the history of the cemetery as well as its importance in our community.

Dave Obee
Victoria, B.C., February 2008

A burial park, not just a cemetery

On a windy day in the late fall of 1923, a few dozen people gathered on a hillside just off East Saanich Road to dedicate a new cemetery. Elected officials from Victoria and Saanich, local ministers and special guests witnessed the end of a process that had taken several years, but that promised to ease the pending shortage of space to bury the dead.

On Wednesday, November 28, 1923, Royal Oak Burial Park in Saanich was declared open. Two days later, a woman named Florence Mary Johns became the first person buried there.

More than 65,000 people have followed. Another 80,000 people have been cremated at Royal Oak.

When it was developed, Royal Oak Burial Park was surrounded by farmland. Today, the farms are gone. The evolution of the area is reflected in the fact that the cemetery has had three addresses — on East Saanich Road, the Patricia Bay Highway and Falaise Drive – without ever moving.

While the burial park is not the oldest in Greater Victoria, it is nevertheless rich with history. Its crematorium has received special recognition as well; built for just $16,000 in the 1930s, it is considered to be one of the finest examples of the Art Deco architectural style on Vancouver Island.

That historic building helped make Royal Oak Burial Park a key factor in the rising popularity of cremations. The cremation rate on southern Vancouver Island has been the highest in North America for years. By the end of the twentieth century, for every person given a conventional burial, nine were cremated.

From the start, Royal Oak was not meant to be just a cemetery; it was designed to serve as a park as well. Today, the burial park takes in about 135 acres, almost double its original size of 80 acres. So far, only about 65 acres have been developed, and plans call for about 25 acres to remain in a natural state forever.

The burial park is managed by the Board of Cemetery Trustees of Greater Victoria, a body established by the City of Victoria and the District of Saanich in 1922. The board has six volunteer directors, three from Victoria and three from Saanich. The cemetery is operated as a not-for-profit corporation, receives no tax subsidy from either of its stakeholder municipalities and is entirely self-financed with all revenues used solely for the benefit of the burial park.

Royal Oak provides perpetual maintenance. A portion of the fee collected for every lot and for every form of memorial is invested into a care fund. The interest covers the cost of the care and maintenance of interment and memorial sites. The care fund is not used for development or capital expenses not related to maintenance. All development, operations and care costs are recovered through fees charged for products and services offered.

Royal Oak Burial Park provides services to all persons regardless of race, colour, religion, or any other categorization.

• The Garden Chapel at Royal Oak Burial Park has been in operation since 1937.

• An aerial view of Royal Oak Burial Park in about 1928. At the time, the driveway to the cemetery was on East Saanich Road.

After years of debate, a decision

Royal Oak Burial Park was the fourth public cemetery set up in the Victoria area after the establishment of Fort Victoria in 1843.

Many earlier burial areas have been discovered throughout the region. Burial cairns were used by the aboriginal peoples who had been living here for hundreds of years. Human bones have been discovered in several areas. Early First Nations often left their dead on small islands or suspended in trees. Later, they started burial grounds adjacent to Lime Bay and at Point Hope.

The first cemetery opened after the Hudson's Bay Company built Fort Victoria in 1843 was just north of the fort, at the southwest corner of Johnson and Douglas streets. The cemetery was for the burial of deceased employees, naval personnel and others, and was shown as "old graveyard" on Lot No. 431 on the first plan of the city, dated July 19, 1858.

The second cemetery was established after commercial development started to push against the borders of the original one. The Johnson Street cemetery was ordered closed, and land was allocated on the church reserve property east of Quadra Street, just north of Christ Church Cathedral. The new cemetery was opened in 1859, with most of the bodies from Johnson Street exhumed and reburied in the Quadra cemetery.

The Quadra cemetery, used throughout the 1860s and into the 1870s, became the final resting place of naval men, employees of the Hudson's Bay Company and a few pioneer merchants. One of the notables buried there is Joseph Austen, a member of the San Francisco vigilantes who came to Victoria in the 1850s and served as a sheriff. He died on July 2, 1871.

Funerals from Esquimalt came by water. The bodies were landed at the old Hudson's Bay Company wharf, with corteges headed by detachments from the naval and military forces.

In 1874, the British Colonist newspaper said that 2,000 interments had taken place at the Quadra cemetery before it was closed in February 1873. After its closure, it fell into a state of disrepair for many years. It was transferred to the city of Victoria for park purposes in 1908. Headstones were collected and placed in rows along the eastern border.

The site for the third cemetery was picked by the City of Victoria, which had been founded in 1862. To follow the Quadra location, the city wanted a larger parcel of land, preferably one not quite so close to downtown. In 1872 the cemetery board recommended a site in the James Bay area that was known as Medana's Grove and was bounded by Dallas Road, Oswego, Niagara and Menzies streets. Local residents were not impressed, however, and the idea faded away. Attention turned instead to the Ross Bay area, east of downtown, and a deal for land there was signed in September.

The first burial in Ross Bay Cemetery was in December, 1872, when Mary Pearse, the wife of government official Benjamin Pearse, was interred. The cemetery was officially opened in March 1873. At first, about 100 people a year were buried there, but the rate slowly rose to about 500 a year by the 1920s. By 1923, when Royal Oak Burial Park was opened, 17,215 people had been buried in Ross Bay Cemetery. Today, about 28,000 are there.

The Ross Bay register contains the names of such well-known pioneers as Sir James Douglas, second governor of Vancouver Island, who died in 1877; Sir Matthew Baillie Begbie, the noted judge, who died in 1894; Amor De Cosmos, who founded the British Colonist newspaper in 1858 and died in 1897; members of the Dunsmuir family; and many other pioneers of Victoria and elsewhere.

Ross Bay was also used by Chinese immigrants, although they were restricted to less-desirable areas of the cemetery, and were often identified by numerals only. The Chinese Consolidated Benevolent Association opened its own cemetery at Harling Point, east of Foul Bay, in 1903.

Ross Bay Cemetery's location, on the shore of Juan de Fuca Strait, was certainly scenic — but it was far from perfect. Its capacity was too small to meet the needs of the growing community. The lower area of the cemetery, close to the water, was at the mercy of the weather.

On January 18, 1908, Victoria's Daily Colonist reported

that winter storms had destroyed much of the cemetery fence next to the bay. In some areas trees had fallen on it, and in other areas the ground had been washed out from underneath it. Many caskets had been exposed to the waves, and pieces were found in the driftwood on the beach.

Local residents claimed to have found bones among the debris, although the Colonist reporter said he saw none. Most of the caskets destroyed were apparently from the graves of Chinese immigrants but there was little to identify the bits of wood. The Colonist warned that higher parts of the cemetery were also at risk. The sea was undercutting the land, it said, tearing away the earth from the roots of the trees and shrubs.

Two months later, the newspaper reported that more waves driven by high winds had ripped into the waterfront, causing it to slide away and expose more caskets.

The problems continued for several years. In January 1910, for example, another gale ripped more caskets out of the ground. The Colonist reported that six had been lost, and that the coping of a tombstone was found on the beach below the graveyard. The newspaper urged that something be done as soon as possible. In response, the city of Victoria ordered that a seawall be built. The work was carried out in 1912 and 1913, and many graves were moved farther inland to make the construction possible.

Stopping the erosion at Ross Bay would solve the immediate concerns. In the long term, however, the city needed to find another site for a cemetery. Victoria city council members looked for a location and talked about how to operate a new cemetery, but made no progress.

Potential relief came from the private sector. In 1916, Victoria city council was approached by Victoria lawyer Frank Higgins, representing the Mountain View Development Company and the Mountain View Burial Company. Higgins had an option on 23 acres on Lansdowne Road and proposed to put a privately owned and operated cemetery on the site. Single plots would go for $20 each, and Higgins promised perpetual upkeep.

Councillors embraced the business model proposed by Higgins, but did not like the notion that a private company would be in charge of what they considered to be a municipal responsibility. As a result, the plan went nowhere.

In August 1918, the councils of Victoria, Esquimalt, Oak Bay and Saanich, along with the local militia, set up a joint committee to try to find a site for a new cemetery. The plan was for the city to buy the property, with all of the interested parties sharing the cost of the maintenance.

Soon, Victoria council was ready to purchase land in the Mount Tolmie area, but opposition killed the deal. That fall, council members decided to put the matter to voters as part of the January 1919 civic election. The referendum failed, possibly because voters did not hear a consistent message. It seemed that council had not yet come up with a clear plan of action.

Six weeks before the referendum, for example, the preferred choice was identified as a 100-acre parcel on Carey Road owned by Dr. Edward Griffiths, a local dentist. But with two weeks to go, council reached a tentative deal on 94 acres from the Tod farm in the Cedar Hill district, south of Mount Douglas.

It got worse. A week before the vote, city authorities revealed that while the proposed bylaw, if approved, would authorize an expenditure of just $37,600, the full cost of the cemetery would be about $100,000. The lower amount was said to be the cost of the land alone.

Voters were not impressed. They rejected the cemetery proposal with 1,917 against it and only 389 in favour, even though civic politicians had told them that Ross Bay had only enough capacity to last another year.

By the end of 1919, two new private proposals were placed in front of the local councils.

The Victoria Daily Times featured an extensive interview with C. Hiram Babcock, a Victoria resident who had most recently been the superintendent of Riverside Memorial Park in Spokane, Washington. He had also worked as a cemetery architect and manager in California, Nevada and Alaska.

Babcock proposed that a modern lawn and park cemetery should be established in a central location and that it should have room for future additions – namely a crematorium, a columbarium to hold cremated remains, and a mausoleum, a building with burial crypts.

SKELETONS ARE SPORT OF GALE

Heavy Seas Wreck Graves on Oak Bay Cemetery Foreshore

Strewn along the cemetery foreshore, at that point where the full force of a southwest gale heaps up with erosive and devastating effect the waters of Ross Bay, are fragments of coffins torn from the shelving bank with the ruthlessness of primeval violence, and scattered broadcast, epitomizing the "vandalism" of natural laws, and furnishing a weird commentary on conditions which can exist amid a civilized community. Further investigations made by the Colonist at Ross Bay cemetery reveal a state of affairs which demands immediate rectification.

Warnings of what would occur when heavy gales were experienced on the coast have been frequently made in the Colonist, which has done everything possible to prevent a state of affairs which is a disgrace to the city. The prognostications made of what would happen in the failure of preventative measures have been verified to the letter. Six coffins at least, containing the bodies or skeletons of those whose memories are highly prized by present residents of the city, have become the sport of wind or water. On the beach also lies the coping of a tombstone, erected in loving memory of some former Victorian.

Yesterday three of the remaining graves, lying in close proximity to the wind and water swept bank, were removed to safer positions. But others are still in immediate danger. A breadth of bank measuring some fifteen feet has collapsed before the sea's incursions which carried away coffins, washing human remains into the tide. For a distance of 400 feet the planking on the effete breakwater has been carried away, bare piles standing to stem the full force of a wind lashed sea.

• From the Daily Colonist, January 21, 1910

He said the demand for cremations was bound to increase, and it made more sense to have a central, local crematorium than for each undertaker to build their own, or for them to ship bodies to Seattle, the site of the nearest crematorium. He also said that there would be demand for crypts in a community mausoleum.

Babcock said a burial park should offer perpetual care, with a percentage from the sale of lots and graves set aside to pay for their maintenance. He lobbied for a uniform plan for the grounds, and argued that tight controls on the design of markers would reduce the cost of upkeep by 50 per cent.

He proposed that management be in the hands of a board of directors. Babcock argued that every organization involved in disposing of the dead, including municipalities, churches, funeral homes and civic organizations, should have a share of the cemetery and be involved in its operation.

Babcock wanted to put the cemetery on the George Rogers property close to the north end of Quadra Street. His plan had the support of the Anglican Synod and two local funeral homes. It was rejected by Saanich council, however, based on council's stand that any cemetery in Saanich should be municipally, not privately, owned and operated.

The other private proposal came from Frank Higgins. He said his new plan called for a private cemetery on 50 acres in the Blenkinsop Valley, west of Mount Douglas, owned by Adam Glendinning. Higgins told Saanich council that the new burial park would not be near any residential area. He also stressed his experience with cemeteries, noting that he was one of the people behind a new cemetery in Vancouver.

He received the same answer that Babcock did — that any new cemetery in Saanich would be operated by the municipality. Higgins argued his case, citing Saanich bylaws that specified only that the municipality would need to approve a new cemetery, not that it would have to be the owner. Saanich council was not swayed. It rejected the proposal from Higgins just as it had rejected Babcock's.

The year of 1920 saw local politicians spend a lot of time talking about a cemetery, but the talk did not translate into action.

In January 1920, Victoria Mayor Robert Porter said the need for a new cemetery was becoming more acute, and that the subject should go to voters as soon as possible. He noted that there had been many previous attempts to set up a new cemetery, starting with John Teague, who had been mayor in 1894 and 1895. Teague had advocated a cemetery in the Cedar Hill area.

The next month, council members from Victoria and Saanich met to discuss cemetery proposals, and remained convinced that municipal ownership was the only approach worth taking. They remained firm despite plans submitted by Higgins, who was now talking of a private cemetery in Colwood, and Babcock, who still wanted to create a private cemetery on land owned by George Rogers. Babcock drafted a plan for the property and submitted it to Saanich council.

Hector Cowper, the municipal clerk in Saanich, recommended that a cemetery trust be established to borrow money for burial park development. Demand for plots would be so great, he said, that there would be no problem paying off the debt almost as soon as the cemetery opened. The Saanich and Victoria councillors liked what Cowper had to say, and decided to invite their counterparts from Oak Bay and Esquimalt to get in on the deal.

A week later, the Cowper proposal was formally endorsed by the inter-municipal committee, made up of members of the councils of the four municipalities in Greater Victoria. The committee asked the provincial government to pass a bill that would allow the creation of a cemetery board.

Progress was finally being made, it seemed. That bill was presented to the legislature in April by George Bell, the government member for Victoria. It would allow a municipality, or group of municipalities, to create a board to acquire land, to borrow money, and to operate a cemetery.

Almost immediately, Bell's bill was "regretfully interred," as the Victoria Daily Times reported on April 16. Premier John Oliver said the proposed bill was not properly drafted, and other members said it was incomplete.

Victoria Mayor Robert Porter declared that his city would develop a cemetery on its own rather than work with the other municipalities. He said the matter would be put before the voters at the next municipal election. Porter also said the city had several possible sites in mind, but did not have a preferred choice. In response, Saanich council renewed its commitment to a public cemetery that would be developed jointly with the other municipalities.

In August, Esquimalt councillors expressed frustration with the slow progress, and said their municipality might need to develop its own cemetery. One councillor suggested solving the problem by setting up a crematorium as soon as possible.

By December, members of the local councils were not only working together, but had found a potential site. They toured William J. Rowland's 80-acre parcel on Tillicum Road near Carey Road, and declared it to be better than any site previously considered.

That prompted Babcock to become involved once again. He said the Rowland land had been offered to him as well, but he had decided against it because of the problems developing it. Only half of it could be used without explosives, he said.

"A man will dig and fill one grave a day on the average in suitable ground for cemetery purposes. If he were paid $5 per day and he digs 700 graves in one acre of ground, the digging of those graves would cost $3,500," Babcock said in a letter to Victoria council. "If the expense of digging 700 graves was doubled on account of encountering hard clay, hard pan or rock, the cost of the land would be increased $3,500 per acre."

The real estate agents handling the Tod property near Mount Douglas protested as well. They said that council had deemed their property to be the prime choice the previous year, and argued that it should still be considered the first choice. The land would be cheaper per acre, they said, than the Rowland property.

Undeterred, Victoria council decided to spend $100 to drill test holes on the Rowland property. Babcock tried to address the council meeting, but the mayor shouted at him to sit down. Aldermen started snarling at each other as well, with accusations made about the lack of progress.

Alderman Edwyn Andros was especially critical of calculations that showed that Ross Bay Cemetery could be used for at least four more years. "Here is a scheme," he said, "in which you try to estimate the number of deaths as a mathematical certainty, by adding and subtracting and multiplying, and all that sort of thing. You simply can't do it. We don't know who is going to die. I don't know where I'm going to die, especially if I continue to associate with you people here."

One month later, in January 1921, council was handed a report by its cemetery committee. The report listed eight possible sites, and rejected all but one of them. The sites were:

• The Waterhouse property, 18 acres near Langford. Rejected because of the distance from the city and the small amount of land.

• The McCrea property, 35 acres in total. The price was deemed to be too high.

• Simon Fraser Tolmie's estate. No price was given, but the land was rejected because of the difficulty of draining it.

• Josiah Bull's 23 acres near Elk Lake. Half the land was deemed unsuitable.

• The Tod estate, rejected in the 1919 referendum. Once council's top choice, it was now deemed to be too far from the city, and it had drainage problems as well.

• Rowland's 50 acres at Burnside Road and Tillicum Road. Considered to be too wet.

• Land between Carey and Tillicum, with lots of rock and swamp, was considered unsuitable.

• Rowland's 50 acres on the east side of Tillicum, just north of the railway tracks — part of the land that council had considered in December. It was praised for its soil and proximity to street car lines, paved streets and water mains. It was the only one to win the committee's endorsement.

In February, a delegation from Victoria and Saanich again asked the provincial government for a bill that would allow the creation of a cemetery board serving more than one municipality. This time, the act passed the test. Championed in the legislature by Liberal member Joseph Badenoch Clearihue, the bill — the Municipal Cemeteries Act — received wide support. Premier John Oliver gave it his blessing after receiving assurances that the religious denomination of dead people would not affect their right to be buried.

With the legalities out of the way, Victoria council members were able to get back to arguing. In May, they could not agree on how much longer the Ross Bay Cemetery could last, or whether unused portions of the cemetery were even suitable for burials. There was general agreement, at least, that much of Ross Bay should not be used for burials during the wet winter months.

Esquimalt council came on board, but with thin support

• Joseph Badenoch Clearihue.
Times Colonist

for the idea of a joint cemetery. The only thing that Esquimalt councillors could agree on was that Ross Bay would soon be full, a notion that was still being debated by their counterparts in Victoria.

That same month, the untiring Babcock came back with a new proposal. He wanted to set up a cemetery on land owned by George Rogers in the Royal Oak area, opposite Josiah Bull's residence. The site would have 33,000 salable burial plots, he said, along with space for a crematorium, a mausoleum and a columbarium. Babcock had already received a commitment that the Lake Hill Motor Bus Line would extend its route to the north to serve his cemetery.

Babcock said he could develop 10,000 spaces immediately, with the rest to come as needed. He said he could look after the surveying and planning, development of roads, landscaping, installation of a water service, construction of a gateway, and fencing for the grand total of $100,000. He also asked to become the cemetery manager for a term of five years. Babcock's offer was referred to the inter-municipal committee for discussion.

The same day that Babcock made his offer, Thomas Purdey, Victoria's parks superintendent, told council that Ross Bay had just 635 plots remaining. With 600 deaths a year in Greater Victoria, the pending crunch was undeniable.

On May 19, the inter-municipal committee adopted a draft agreement that called for the involvement of all four municipalities in Greater Victoria, and a limit of $150,000 in borrowing. Saanich clerk Cowper said the amount of land purchased should be no more than 40 acres, in order to keep costs down. That would, he said, meet the region's burial needs for 30 years.

Babcock attended the meeting. His proposal was not discussed then, but a few days later it came in for harsh criticism from another side. Major H. Cuthbert Holmes, who had represented the Chamber of Commerce at the committee meeting, told a gathering of chamber members that he was not impressed. Holmes noted that Babcock had said it would take just 60 days to set up a new cemetery. Since Ross Bay could handle burials for at least 18 more months, Holmes said, there was no rush to establish a new cemetery.

Victoria council approved an agreement to set up an inter-municipal cemetery board, with two representatives from the city and one each from Saanich, Esquimalt and Oak Bay. Costs would be split between the municipalities based on population numbers. Some Victoria councillors expressed concern about signing a deal that would not give the city a majority on the board, but finally relented.

The deal lasted just two months, falling apart when both Oak Bay and Esquimalt pulled out. Oak Bay said the operation of the cemetery should be up to the city and the municipality where the cemetery would be located – and clearly, that would not be Oak Bay. Esquimalt cited problems getting information from Victoria and Saanich.

That left Victoria and Saanich councils to work out the terms of a new agreement. In September, a joint meeting resulted in a tentative deal to have a six-person cemetery board, with three members from each municipality. Saanich and Victoria would also share equally in the financial commitments. The committee was authorized to borrow up to $100,000, which was $50,000 less than the amount that had been proposed if all four municipalities had agreed to take part. The two councils left open the door for Esquimalt and Oak Bay to join the project later.

Victoria Mayor William Marchant urged a quick start to the work, noting once again that Ross Bay Cemetery was getting full. As a side argument, he said the project would provide jobs for the unemployed men of the region.

In December, Saanich Reeve George Watson said the deal would be a good one for the municipality, and noted the keen interest of private developers was a sign that a cemetery would be a good investment.

His message, quite simply, was that men such as Babcock were not philanthropists, they were businessmen out to make money – money that could go to the municipality instead.

The cemetery proposal was put to voters in Saanich in January 1922. It was approved, with 1,391 voters in favour and 417 opposed. Victoria council, which had gone to the voters and lost three years earlier, did not take the chance of another referendum failing. It simply gave its blessing to the plan.

With the tough decisions out of the way, the councils were ready to create the board that would run the much-needed new cemetery.

Following Seattle's example

In February 1922, representatives from Saanich and Victoria did further fine-tuning to their agreement. They decided that the cemetery committee could borrow up to $80,000. They also reiterated that the other municipalities would be welcome to join later if desired.

By this time, Victoria alderman Reginald Hayward had become the deal's keenest advocate on Victoria city council. He doubtless had a strong interest in burial space, because he ran the funeral home that had been started by his father 55 years earlier.

Saanich councillors had no problem with the cemetery agreement, but the ones from Victoria were concerned that there was no provision for the continuing maintenance of Ross Bay Cemetery, and that Victoria council would have no say in the choice of a cemetery site. Hayward told his fellow councillors that the legislation under which the cemetery board was created would make it impossible for the board to look after Ross Bay. Besides, he said, the board had to ensure that it set aside enough money for perpetual maintenance of burial plots, and at the same time build up a fund to pay for an additional cemetery that would be needed once the new cemetery was full.

"It would be quite reasonable to leave Ross Bay Cemetery out of the question," Hayward said. "To maintain Ross Bay after it became non-self-supporting, the purchasers of plots in the new burial park would not only have to pay a price sufficient to maintain the new cemetery, but also an additional cost to maintain the old, in which they had no interest, which to my idea would be unjust."

Hayward said that Victoria council could not pick the cemetery location, as that would violate the act. He said the cemetery board trustees would include members of Victoria council, and those people would surely look out for Victoria's interests.

Both councils signed the deal on March 16, creating the Board of Cemetery Trustees of Greater Victoria. The first trustees were Victoria Mayor Marchant and two aldermen, Hayward and R.W. Perry, as well as Saanich Reeve George F. Watson and councillors George McWilliam and Albert Edward Horner.

The trustees held their first meeting on March 29. They picked Hayward as their chairman and Hector Cowper, the Saanich clerk who had devised the financing plan, as their secretary. One of their decisions was to call for tenders for the land they would need. They also decided that a small committee should visit model cemeteries in other cities, looking for ideas to use in Victoria.

In the first week of April, Hayward and three other members of the cemetery board — Watson, Perry and McWilliam — left the Island to visit seven cemeteries in Vancouver, Seattle, Tacoma and Spokane. The tour included Vancouver's newest cemetery, Ocean View Burial Park, which had opened in October 1919, as well as Spokane's Riverside, which had been managed by Hiram Babcock.

The committee members reported that they were most impressed with Evergreen Cemetery, a relatively new cemetery on the north side of Seattle. It was designed as a burial park rather than a cemetery. Upright monuments were not permitted, so the grounds had more uniformity and beauty.

As a result, Evergreen became the model used by the Greater Victoria trustees.

In April, the cemetery board placed advertisements in the Colonist and the Times, with the headline Cemetery Site Wanted. The ads said the board wanted from 30 to 80 acres, and that preference would be given to a site with sandy subsoil, with access to a good road, within reasonable distance of a water supply, and with "features that could lend to its beautification."

The board warned that it would ask for a 30-day option, as well as the right to enter the property to test the soil. Offers had to be submitted to the board by April 18.

On April 19, the day after the deadline, trustees met to draft a more stringent list of requirements, based in large part on what Hayward's committee had seen at Evergreen in Seattle. The Colonist itemized the new wish list:

"1. That the site to be purchased be of rolling nature,

• Seattle's Evergreen Cemetery was still quite new when the Victoria delegation arrived. Its first burial had been in July 1920, less than two years earlier. Originally planned as a housing development on the North Trunk Highway — Aurora Avenue — Evergreen was privately owned, but set up as an "endowment care" cemetery. Part of the cost of a grave goes into a trust fund for maintenance of the grounds.

Evergreen has evolved over the years. A few years after the Vancouver Island councillors visited, it was combined with the cemetery across the street, and its name has been changed to Evergreen-Washelli.

The cemetery has more than 145,000 graves, making it the largest cemetery in Washington state. But with more than 5,000 upright white marble veterans' markers, it can no longer be considered to be free of monuments.

and if possible of sandy sub-soil.

"2. That offers of flat land be not considered until all sites of the above type are first dealt with.

"3. That no site of less than 30 acres be purchased, and preferably nearer 50 acres, if finances permit.

"4. That in the event of a site being selected, that only from five to 10 acres be developed immediately.

"5. That no main roadways be constructed less than 20 feet within the park, and no roadways of any kind less than 16 feet.

"6. That pathways, which shall be of grass, be not less than six feet wide, and parallel to each other.

"7. That only a limited number of monuments in specified sections be permitted, and on ground of a size to be determined later, and all monuments to be on a base level with the ground.

"8. That on family and single plots, flat granite or marble slabs of a regulation size be permitted, to be set in regulation situation, to be determined later, and these to be flush with the ground.

"9. That all plots be marked by the superintendent with a concrete marker, bearing the name of the deceased, the cost of same to be included in the sale price of the plot. Marker to be flush with the ground.

"10. That all plots be marked out with concrete stakes, set flush, bearing number of the plot. Stake to be from 10 to 12 inches long.

"11. That all graves, including indigent, be subject to perpetual maintenance.

"12. That a competent man with technical knowledge of cemeteries be employed at the proper time to plan and lay out the site as a burial park.

"13. That if possible to get a person such as required in No. 12, who could carry on at a reasonable salary as superintendent, whose duty it would be, among others, to carry out the future development of the cemetery as required, that such a person be sought for as soon as the site is decided upon."

With that, the board members opened the tenders that had been submitted in response to the ad. They reported that there were 19 offers, with prices ranging from $85 an acre to $1,000. Some of the land offered was cleared and cultivated,

• Reginald Hayward.
Times Colonist

and some was still partly timbered.

A decision came quickly. A couple of weeks after tenders closed, the board members rejected all 19 offers, saying the prices being asked were excessively high. Now, the board said that asking prices had ranged from $600 to $1,500 an acre.

The failure to find a suitable, affordable site was just a minor setback. The board simply decided to rescind one of its first resolutions — the one requiring tenders for the land. Instead, the board members would be allowed to start private negotiations with owners of sites deemed suitable for a cemetery, including one at Cadboro Bay.

That idea raised a few fears and rumours in the community. Six influential businessmen, including the manager of the Uplands development in north Oak Bay, fired off a letter to the Colonist designed to discourage the cemetery board from looking in that area. "Cadboro Bay — one of Victoria's greatest assets — is in danger of being converted from a playground into a cemetery," the letter said. "The $80,000 voted for the purchase of a cemetery site may be used to destroy an asset that could not be bought for 10 times the money. How any public trustee could even consider such a scheme for a single moment passes all comprehension — but so it is.

"Out of all the miles of hinterland where the necessary, but gloomy, institution might be established, they must not choose one of our most beautiful playgrounds and dump a city of the dead right down in the very middle of it," the letter said. The Royal Victoria Yacht Club, the Canadian Club and the Victoria and Island Publicity Bureau also appealed directly to the cemetery board to forget about any plans for Cadboro Bay. Several petitions were raised.

Those concerns, along with the high price apparently being asked for the Cadboro Bay property, prompted the cemetery trustees to look elsewhere.

The trustees received revised offers on eight of the original 19 parcels of land, as well as a new proposal for property at Langford. They quickly narrowed the list to three sites, and asked that an engineer be consulted regarding their suitability. One of the final three offers came from Hiram Babcock, who was still trying to develop land owned by George Rogers.

In May 1922, the Colonist published an essay by Babcock on the planning and designing of burial lawn parks. He said the selection of a site was a task that called for "knowledge and experience," and that an "expert landscape gardener and designer" would be needed once the site was picked.

"In all modern burial grounds the lawn-park system is invariably adopted," Babcock wrote. "The old conception of an unsightly graveyard gives place to the nobler conception of a magnificent park, where the beloved departed may rest forever midst beauteous nature at her best." The Colonist included a map of Babcock's proposed plan for a burial park in Victoria.

Babcock's position reflected the latest thinking on cemetery design. The popular belief at the time was that a cemetery could be something more than just a plot of land filled with markers – it could also serve as a park, or a garden, or a recreational area. Cemetery experts in North America and England argued that devoting a site to just the burial of the dead was a waste of space and opportunity.

The board pressed forward, hiring engineer Frederick Butterfield to inspect and report on the proposed cemetery sites. On May 19, the board was approached by the real estate company of Carlow and McElhoes, offering 84.1 acres in Section 109 of the Lake District — in layman's terms, on the east side of East Saanich Road, just north of Royal Oak. On June 5, Butterfield was asked to submit a report on that land, which was owned by the Mycock family. Fifty test holes and three test graves were dug.

Within four days, Butterfield gave his blessing to the Mycock land. The trustees quickly offered the Mycocks $200 an acre, pending approval by the District of Saanich and the Provincial Board of Health. The Mycocks accepted, agreeing to sell the property for $16,820.

Hayward said the deal represented a saving of $28,000 from what the board would have had to spend if it had accepted any of the original 19 offers. The lower cost was possible because the land was cheaper than what was originally offered, less money would have to be spent on improvements, and less would have to be spent on maintenance.

He said that $40,000 in cemetery debentures would go on sale immediately. Proceeds would be used to buy the land and start the work on developing the site.

The Mycock property was reported to be one of the highest on the Saanich Peninsula, with views of Juan de Fuca Strait. It was described as resembling a corrugated saucer with natural drainage to the centre. Ridges and heavy stands of timber meant that most of the burial plots would not be seen from East Saanich Road. The knolls and depressions would become part of the cemetery design.

Hayward said that portions of the land were natural parkland, and the part that could not be used for burials would be kept as park-like as possible.

In an attempt to ease any concerns about the location of the new cemetery, which was six miles from city hall, Hayward said that the board was considering how people would get there from Victoria. If private bus companies did not step forward, he said, the board might run its own transportation system. Also, he noted, the cemeteries serving Seattle, Tacoma and Vancouver were all farther from the city than the Mycock land was from Victoria. Not only that, he said, but Ross Bay Cemetery had also been dismissed at one time as being too far from the city.

Hayward said the new cemetery would not be filled for at least 60 years. A second entrance would be added later. Hayward also promised that a lily pond would be created in the centre of the cemetery. In a 1967 interview with the Colonist, former Saanich councillor Albert Edward Horner, an original member of the cemetery board, said that the original concept included not only a pond but a stone bridge as well.

Both the pond and the bridge disappeared from the plans before construction started. Rather than use water as a beautifying feature, the designers did their best to hide it. Much of Normandy Creek, a tributary of Colquitz River that originates on burial park land, was buried in a culvert. The creek's little valley was filled in to create more room for plots.

Henry Esson Young, the provincial officer of health, gave his blessing to the site. Albert Edward Horner told the Colonist that after that, the $16,820 payment was made to the Mycocks in cold, hard cash, with a police escort ensuring that the money made it safely.

Babcock tried once again to get involved. In July, he applied for the job of laying out the new cemetery, and included a letter of reference from Riverside Park Cemetery in Spokane, among other documents. The board simply returned

• Lake District land records show that the first owner of the Royal Oak Burial Park property was Paul Medana, who made his first payment on the land on August 1, 1859. Medana – whose substantial land holdings in James Bay had been considered for a cemetery in the early 1870s, before Ross Bay was selected – died in November 1868 and is buried in the Quadra Street cemetery.

Medana's Royal Oak land was later taken over by the Heal family, with the Crown grant issued to Julia Heal on March 13, 1878. The original parcel was 135 acres and extended as far south as today's Royal Oak Drive. The Heals subdivided the property in the late 1890s, and by 1904 Henry Mycock was listed in the tax rolls as the owner of the northern portion.

Henry and Rachel Mycock were from England, and also lived in Australia before coming to Canada. The family lived for about 15 years in the Lake Hill area before moving to the Royal Oak farm.

The Mycock family lived on the Royal Oak farm for 18 years. They used it for pasturage, with some of the land seeded to grain and fodder crops.

those testimonials to him.

One problem with the Mycock land was that it did not have direct access to East Saanich Road. The Mycocks had been crossing land owned by their neighbours, but the amount of traffic that a cemetery would generate called for a more formal solution.

In August, trustees voted to buy more land in order to provide a proper entrance. Two months later, they completed a deal with John Caven, who owned one of the lots between the Mycock land and East Saanich Road. The board paid $400 for about three-quarters of an acre on the south edge of Caven's property, giving the new cemetery room for the road access that it needed. The Caven land had previously been owned by two Saanich pioneers, Richard Cheeseman and his son-in-law Joseph Goyette.

The board hired the Seattle firm of Gardiner, Gardiner and Fischer to help design the cemetery. A.S. Fischer, one of the principals of the consulting firm, and engineer Butterfield drafted a report on the site on October 25, 1922.

They said the cemetery land was made up of three enclosed valleys, one of which was similar to an amphitheatre. Portions of the site were too rocky to be considered for burials, but that had been taken into account in the total price. On the other hand, a large portion of the site had been under cultivation for many years, which meant it would be cheap to develop for a cemetery.

The report said that roads should be kept as close to the valley bottoms as possible. This would allow for the most artistic, natural development, with burial plots above the roads. Butterfield and Fischer included cost estimates based on those incurred by Evergreen Cemetery in Seattle. Their projection of revenue was based on the average number of burials at Ross Bay over the previous five years — 540 — and the belief that once the new cemetery opened, there would be no more burials at Ross Bay.

They recommended that a new house be built for the cemetery superintendent, who would be expected to observe the approach of funeral processions and guide them to the proper spot. The old Mycock farm house, they said, would not be suitable. The board agreed, saying that the Mycock house could be used as an office during construction, and could double as a sleeping area at night, but should be removed after that. A new house, to be built just inside the cemetery gates on the old Caven land, was approved.

The board decided that half of the cemetery employees should be taxpayers in Victoria, and the other half taxpayers in Saanich.

Progress made over the winter of 1922-23 included office work, the preparation of plans regarding the sizes of plots, lengths, frontage, and the drainage and irrigation schemes. The pay for construction workers was initially set at $3.20 for an eight-hour day, with employees responsible for getting to and from the site. In January 1923 the scale was expanded. Ordinary labour would still get $3.20 a day, but rockmen would get $3.45, blacksmiths $3.50, and teams of horses $6.40.

The Victoria and District Trades and Labour Council complained that the amount paid was too low. The cemetery board argued in response that the wages were similar to what was being paid by other employers, so they would not be raised.

By the summer of 1923, up to sixty men at a time were busy reshaping the property, especially the first six and a half acres to be used for burials. A key part of the work was the creation of a drainage system, including the enclosure of the creek. A water main service complete with standpipes was built. Crews used rock from a quarry in the southeast corner of the cemetery property to build a mile and a half of roads

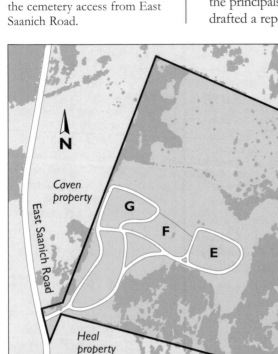

• Royal Oak Burial Park in 1923, with the first three sections identified.
Extra land was bought to give the cemetery access from East Saanich Road.

twenty-two feet wide. These roads were oil-surfaced at first, with asphalt added a few years later. Water service had to be brought to the site, and electrical lines were strung from Wilkinson Road to the cemetery.

By August Butterfield said the initial work would be finished by September. It would then be ready for seeding and boulevarding. The appearance of the cemetery at the time was plain. The reshaping of the land had prompted the removal of all trees in the sections to be used for graves, and since no new trees had been planted in their place, the ground looked quite empty.

The board placed a help wanted ad in the local papers, looking for someone who would serve as both gardener and superintendent in exchange for $125 a month and the use of a modern bungalow with free water. The successful applicant was John Thomas Wilkinson, a native of Leeds, Yorkshire, who had worked in the gardens of private estates in England and Wales. He had served as gardener at Government House in Victoria for five years. The board also named Victoria city clerk E.W. Bradley as its secretary-treasurer.

An area in the new cemetery was tentatively set aside for open-air cremations. Immigrants from India, who cremated their dead for religious reasons, would be able to use the rock quarry at the new cemetery rather than a corner of Ross Bay Cemetery as before.

On September 21, 1923, the cemetery was finally given a name: Royal Oak Burial Park. It was simple enough; the location was Royal Oak, and the park-like design meant it was a "burial park" rather than a cemetery.

By October, Butterfield reported that the crew was down to 18 men and one team of horses, and that the steam roller would only be needed for a few more days. The major work that was left was the staking out of roadways and plots. The board set prices at $40 for the grave itself, $7.50 for digging it, $1.50 for the marker and $1 for a vase.

The grand opening of the burial park was on Wednesday, November 28, 1923. Despite a strong wind, about 70 people attended the ceremony on a hill just off East Saanich Road, with a view of the Olympic Mountains in the background. A temporary platform, draped with huge flags, was erected for the event.

A special guest was Clinton S. Harley of the Evergreen cemetery in Seattle, which had been the inspiration for Royal Oak. Another Seattle man, A.S. Fischer, who had been a consulting engineer, was invited but could not attend. If Hiram Babcock was there, his presence was not recorded in the newspapers of the day.

Cemetery board chairman Hayward — Victoria's mayor since the December 1922 civic election — started the ceremony with a brief history of the park. That was followed by the hymn "O God, Our Help in Ages Past"; a scripture reading by Dean Cecil S. Quainton of Christ Church Cathedral; an opening address by Rev. William Stevenson; an opening prayer by Rev. Dr. Wilford J. Sipprell of the Metropolitan Church; and benediction by Rev. Arthur de B. Owen of the Church of Our Lord.

"In the name of the Christian churches and on behalf of the citizens of Victoria and Saanich we hereby dedicate this piece of ground to be known as the Royal Oak Burial Park, where the bodies of our dead may rest in peace and in honoured remembrance 'Until the day break and the shadows flee away'," Stevenson said in his address.

And with that, the years of talking, arguing, planning and construction came to an end. The long-awaited new cemetery was open — and not a moment too soon, given all the talk about Ross Bay running out of space. Three sections in the burial park were ready for interments, and the plans called for more sections to be developed as needed.

The first interment at Royal Oak Burial Park was on Friday, November 30, just two days after the grand opening. Florence Mary Johns of Cowichan Bay, who had died of cancer, was buried in Section F. In December eight more graves were sold at Royal Oak, with interments in five of them.

Greater Victoria's new cemetery was finally in business.

BURIAL PARK HAS NOVEL FEATURES

MODERN CEMETERY IS TO BE OPENED TODAY

Perpetual Upkeep—Only Flat Stones Level With Ground Permitted —First Interment Friday

The Royal Oak Burial Park, which will be officially opened this afternoon with a short ceremony at three o'clock, is an example of the fashion in cemeteries. It is novel to Vancouver Island because:

1—It is called a burial park instead of a cemetery;

2—It has a contour of rolling hills and valleys, with rock and forest included among the assets rather than the detriments;

3—Its system of financing provides for a fund which will pay sufficient interest to allow of perpetual maintenance from the latter alone;

4—The graves will be located in well-kept lawns, and no graves will be neglected;

5—Only flat stones set level with the ground will be permitted on the graves, and no curbings will be allowed;

6—The property is owned by an intermunicipal body made up of representatives of Victoria and Saanich, which municipalities guarantee the bonds of the board.

• From the Daily Colonist, November 28, 1923

• The official opening of Royal Oak Burial Park on Nov. 28, 1923, drew a
crowd to the East Saanich Road location. These people gathered just inside
the cemetery entrance to hear the speeches and sing along with the hymns.

Image I-68726 courtesy of Royal BC Museum, BC Archives

• The platform at the opening of the burial park included, from left, Rev. William Stevenson, Rev. Arthur de B. Owen, Victoria Mayor Reginald Hayward, Victoria Alderman Eugene Sydney Woodward, Rev. A.K. McMinn, Dean Cecil S. Quainton, Rev. John S. Patterson, Saanich Councillor George McWilliam, Rev. Dr. Wilford J. Sipprell, engineer Frederick Butterfield, Saanich Councillor Francis Simpson, Saanich Reeve George Watson, Seattle cemetery manager Clinton S. Harley and Laura Harley.

Image I-68727 courtesy of Royal BC Museum, BC Archives

• On opening day, white stakes were in place in two sections of the cemetery to guide staff members to the location of the plots, as laid out by Frederick Butterfield and his crew.

The hungry years

A crowd started to gather in Royal Oak Burial Park in the early afternoon of Saturday, August 20, 1927. British Columbians wanted to pay their last respects to "Honest" John Oliver, the popular premier who had died in office a few days before.

Oliver's funeral procession moved from the Parliament Building, where his body had been resting, along Government Street to Yates Street, then east to the First United Church for the service. After that, the procession drove north on Quadra Street to East Saanich Road and what the Victoria Daily Times referred to as a "peaceful little burial ground" – Royal Oak Burial Park.

It was an impressive sight. The cortege included police chiefs, a band, members of the provincial Executive Council, the lieutenant-governor, the Speaker of the House, members of the provincial parliament, naval and military officers, senators, judges, members of the House of Commons, representatives of other provincial governments, foreign consuls, municipal representatives, war veterans, and interested members of the public. And flowers – enough to fill five cars.

People gathered along the route to watch the procession go past. It arrived at Royal Oak at 5:30 p.m. Rev. William G. Wilson officiated at the burial service. Rev. James Strachan offered the prayer. Rev. W. Leslie Clay said the benediction as the casket was lowered into the ground.

It was a turning point for Royal Oak Burial Park. It was the largest funeral the young park had witnessed. Oliver was not only the first premier to be interred there, he was a hugely popular one, known as being a man of the people. His selection of Royal Oak over Ross Bay, the cemetery of choice for so many of British Columbia's political leaders, was in keeping with his philosophy about connecting with the common people rather than the elite.

Still, the local newspapers made sure that Oliver's resting place was seen to be special. "The grave is situated in Section G, Lot 195, Grave E," the Daily Colonist reported. "It is in a commanding position on the highest part of the park in the northeast corner."

In the years that followed, other premiers joined Oliver at Royal Oak, taking some of the attention away from him. And a few thousand people were buried farther up the hill, so it could no longer be said that he was the highest. But the arrival of John Oliver was a welcome development for Royal Oak, which had been open less than four years.

The municipal politicians who had pushed so hard for its establishment were already struggling with a nasty surprise. The demand that they had anticipated was not there. The reason? Ross Bay, it turned out, still had plenty of room.

In a review of 1924, the first full year of operation, Saanich Reeve George F. Watson — by then the chairman of the cemetery board — was blunt. "If it had been realized that such a large number of interments were still possible at Ross Bay Cemetery, consideration would have been given to some suspension of the development at Royal Oak," he said.

Watson said only 88 graves at Royal Oak were sold in 1924, with interments in 61 of them. The other 27 were being held in reserve. By comparison, 461 people were buried in Ross Bay Cemetery that year, with 428 in plots sold that year and the rest in plots that had been reserved in earlier years.

It is possible that earlier assessments of the remaining number of plots at Ross Bay had not taken into account the difference between graves used and graves that had simply been reserved. It is clear, however, that hundreds of graves were still available at Ross Bay.

The opening of Royal Oak had an obvious impact on the business being done at Ross Bay. The number of burials at Ross Bay had averaged 526 a year in 1921-23. In 1926-1928, Ross Bay averaged 275 a year, and Royal Oak averaged 301. The problem was that while Royal Oak quickly became responsible for more than half of the region's burials, plans for the burial park had been based on the theory that it would get almost 100

• The entry for Premier John Oliver in the burial park register.

• The first building erected after the burial park opened was this house for the superintendent.

*Image 2006-015-053G
courtesy of Saanich Archives*

per cent of them.

The low-maintenance, plain-memorial policy at Royal Oak Burial Park did not help matters. It might have been less expensive to keep tidy, but people still liked the look of monuments, and wanted to place them on the graves of their loved ones. That made Ross Bay, famous for its large monuments, the preferred resting place for many people.

In 1924, Alexander Stewart and Arthur Mortimer, representing the monument dealers in the city, approached the board to lobby for raised markers. They were told that raised markers would not be allowed. A few months later Mortimer tried again, noting that many plot holders had asked for raised markers. He was again rejected by the board.

Still, there were positive signs. In section G, 109 graves were reserved for ex-servicemen, and others were set aside for members of the Masonic fraternity. The Anglican synod paid $500 as a deposit on the entire section E, and then placed a cross on the hill in the centre of the section.

Development work continued after the burial park was opened. The contract for the superintendent's house went to Donald McKinnon Lindsay, who agreed to do the job for $2,720. The architect was Hubert Savage. A further $45 was approved for a full basement under the house. The board also approved a direct city telephone line for the house, plus a listing in the directory.

Savage also designed the cemetery's entrance, including the iron gates. The board hired stonemason George Davis to build the entrance, using gates provided by James Morrison's machine shop. Hafer Machine Shop of Royal Oak won the $68.50 contract to make the nameplates on the iron railings at the entrance.

Farmer Josiah Bull — who had tried to sell his own land to the cemetery board a few years earlier — leased an unused part of the grounds for five years at $150 a year. He would cover the cost of a fence. The first permanent maintenance employees, James Watt and William Eddie, started work in December 1923. They were paid $95 a month at first, with a raise to $100 a month in 1926.

The board tried to get a special rate from Sidney Flying Line, which ran a bus past the gate. The company said it could not reduce the 35-cent fare each way. The board tried again, and the company said 45 cents for a return trip was the best it could do. The board said this information should be given to the press. The board also imposed a speed limit on vehicles in the park: 10 miles an hour.

The cemetery board was still working out the kinks of its operation when it found itself the subject of sharp criticism.

In 1926, Saanich Reeve Robert Macnicol wrote to the cemetery board to protest that the graves of the poor — buried at the expense of the cemetery board — were not being marked. "So far as Saanich indigents are concerned we do not desire this condition of things to continue," Macnicol said. The cemetery board was firm. If markers were desired, then someone other than the board would have to pay for them.

Macnicol also complained that more than one body had been buried in one of the indigent graves. Within a couple of days, the dispute became ugly. The cemetery board replied to Macnicol that the plot in question was irregular in shape, and could easily handle three bodies. The plot was in a section set aside for indigents, the board said. Beyond that, if the grave contained the bodies of two strangers, the board argued, it could hardly have a marker.

The board then accused Macnicol of having signed a certificate declaring a Saanich woman to be indigent when she was not. The woman had signed her property, worth about $1,000, over to the municipality, and was receiving $15 a month in return.

Macnicol fired back in a letter to the editor of the Colonist. He said the board's refusal to put a marker on the grave was an attempt to deceive the public about its burial of two people in one plot. He repeated his demand that all graves at the cemetery be marked, and said he would ask for the dismissal of board members if they failed to act on his request.

The Colonist trivialized his concerns, saying that Saanich councillors must have no living political issues "when they are striving to make a political issue of the burial of the dead."

Macnicol replied that he would continue his fight until the board agreed to mark all graves. He said that unless his wishes were granted he would ask for the resignation of two Saanich representatives, George Watson and Francis Simpson, for failing to represent the wishes of Saanich. They had argued against marking the indigent graves, while Victoria city council members were willing to go along with it.

In the end, the board decided that all graves would have concrete markers made at the burial park. These could be replaced with fancier, more durable markers if desired. The burial park continued to place the basic markers on graves until the end of the twentieth century, when it was decided to stop the practice because the vast majority of them were being replaced within weeks of being put in the ground.

The burial park was expanded, ever so slightly, in 1928. The board paid Walter Heal, who owned the land to the south of the cemetery, $200 for a 20-foot right-of-way near the entrance. This strip improved access to and from East Saanich Road. The board rejected an offer of the rest of John Caven's land, between the burial park and the road, for $6,000.

The board built a small shelter on the west side of East Saanich Road for the use of people waiting for a bus. It also erected a "public convenience" at a cost of $126. That toilet soon brought protests from people visiting graves nearby.

It was, however, just a minor concern, given the burial park's financial plight. In 1930, board chairman John Harvey optimistically predicted that there would be a large increase in revenue in the years ahead because "the public was starting to recognize the benefits of a modern cemetery." Given the problems the burial park had experienced, Harvey needed to provide some reassurances that the project had been a good idea.

But the 1930s were a tough time for the burial park, along with just about every other organization in Canada. The Great Depression, sparked by the stock market crash in October 1929, was felt even in the cemetery business. Money was not coming in. By June 1931, for example, the trustees had to contact lawyers for advice on what to do about people falling behind on their bills. Some buyers simply abandoned the graves they had reserved.

The board saved money wherever possible. The superintendent was asked to cut costs. His request for a desk was granted — but he was ordered to pay no more than $9 for it, and to buy it from the Red Cross workshop, which provided work for disabled Great War veterans. Requests for many small purchases, such as a mower blade sharpener, were simply tabled.

The issue of the cemetery came up in May 1931 at a meeting of the Victoria Ratepayers' Association. The tough financial situation made the cemetery a target. A speaker criticized the council for many things, including the way "the administration of Mayor Hayward stuck a cemetery on us."

That prompted Hayward, by now an MLA, to write to the editor of the Colonist to counter the claim. He said the burial park had never cost taxpayers a dollar, thanks to the bond issue that was used to finance it. "Royal Oak Burial Park never has been and never will be a source of expense to the taxpayers of Victoria or Saanich," he said.

Hayward also chose to address rumours that the six original cemetery board members had received kickbacks for picking the Mycock site. He noted that the amount paid for the land was so low that if kickbacks had been paid, the Mycocks would likely have received nothing at all. By that time, Henry and Rachel Mycock were no longer worried about allegations or rumours. Both had died, and both had been buried on their former farm, Royal Oak Burial Park.

Along with the Mycocks and Premier John Oliver, the list of people buried at Royal Oak during its early years of operation includes former lieutenant-governor Walter Cameron Nichol; Florence Rattenbury, the first wife of famed architect Francis Rattenbury; former B.C. Premier Simon Fraser Tolmie; and Walter Scott, the first premier of Saskatchewan.

Another burial, that of accountant John Watson in 1931, changed the appearance of the park. Despite the gloomy economic times, Watson's widow Margaretta did what she could to help the park and to remember her husband.

On May 9, 1932, she wrote to the cemetery board, including a sketch of a bird bath. "I would like it to be placed in the said park," she said. "It would be ornamental as well as

Please enform me of your decision after gaining such. I will give Mr. Bennett the order to make the bath. I have viewed his work and think he does good work and this sketch is according to what I think would be appropriate for placing in the park

• Margaretta Watson gave clear instructions with her gift.

a great comfort for the birds." She had already lined up someone to do the work, a man named Bennett.

Watson said she would pay for the bird bath, and offered $100 for its maintenance. She said she would have liked to see it in the Anglican plot – section E, where her husband had been buried the year before – but noted that since that would not be possible, it could go in a small area adjacent to the section.

The trustees unanimously accepted Watson's offer. A few days later, she wrote again, this time enclosing a sketch of a drinking fountain. "This fountain will be constructed of art stone. If your board should desire a spray or anything please say so. Mr. Bennett suggested a stepping stone for little people at the side if necessary."

Watson said that Bennett would make the fountain unique as well as useful. The board unanimously accepted that offer, too. Watson wasn't finished. Along with the bird bath, $100, and the fountain, she donated a $500 bond and six iron forms. In October, she donated shrubs for planting in the soldiers section, and "anywhere else deemed suitable." In January 1933, Watson offered $100 to go toward a small greenhouse. In March, she gave $414 for a small stucco office. Caleb Horspool was hired to build it.

Watson's gifts appear in the burial park's cash book. They stand out; along with regular entries for plot sales (at $40 to $60 each) and vase placements ($1 apiece) there were notations such as this, dated May 25, 1932: "$100 from Mrs. Watson, for the maintenance of a bird bath."

The "Watson Trust Reserve Fund" was listed separately in the cemetery's accounts until the late 1970s, when it was folded into the general maintenance account. In the 1930s, it was a significant factor in the development of the cemetery, which simply could not afford to pay for the beautification of the property. In 1934, the Watson fund – inspired by a single burial – was equivalent to about five per cent of the total main-

tenance reserve that had built up from a decade's worth of interments. Put another way, Watson's cash gifts in 1932 could have covered the burial park's entire payroll for one month.

Others were not as fortunate as Watson. By early 1934, Josiah Bull could no longer pay the rent on the burial park land that he had been farming. He delivered to the burial park half a ton of oats and 1,020 pounds of hay. It was accepted by the board, and his bill was adjusted accordingly. Bull gave up his lease soon after.

In May 1934, the board reached the limit on its borrowing power and could no longer pay its bills. The trustees had to ask both municipalities for $4,000 to help. Victoria and Saanich offered to have development work on the new section done by relief. That did little to resolve the burial park's financial woes; for the rest of the 1930s and into the 1940s, the board repeatedly had to ask its sponsoring councils for financial assistance so it could pay its bills.

Board chairman Henry Clarence Oldfield had a proposal in 1934 that he said would help the burial park cope with the downturn — and at the same time, help the local residents who had to find money to pay for the burials of their loved ones. As the minutes say:

"The chairman proceeded to explain to the meeting that, owing to competition from other cemeteries in the selling of cheap burial plots, the board through such competition is finding difficulty in meeting its financial obligations, and recommended that immediate action be taken to enable us to compete, by setting aside and developing a portion of the burial park for this purpose, and, also that, the board make application to the legislature to have section 18 of the Municipal Cemeteries Act amended in such a way as would enable the plots to be sold in the proposed new section, without having to be perpetually maintained."

In other words, Royal Oak Burial Park would have a discount section. On high ground with trees on two sides, the new section was south of Section D. By the time it was completed in May 1936, it had been given the name D Extension. The 835 plots were initially offered for $15 each. The plan was to maintain the land as long as funds were available, but the section was not to enjoy the same level of perpetual care offered elsewhere in the park. On the other hand, there were no restrictions on the types of headstones that could be used, which gave families a chance to provide raised markers for their loved ones.

That August, it was decided that indigents were to be buried in D Extension. That might have been a practical decision, because the 1936 annual report stated that regular customers had little interest in the area. It turned out that most people preferred to pay a bit extra for the long-term care that was available in other sections.

In September 1937, 50 graves in D Extension were set aside for soldiers who had become government cases.

Much of Section D proper was reserved for members of the Church of England. On May 2, 1937, Bishop Harold Eustace Sexton consecrated the area in a ceremony attended by a large crowd, including Victoria Mayor Andrew McGavin. The choir of St. Michael's Church in Royal Oak led the gathering in the singing of two hymns and a psalm. Afterwards, tea was served in the Royal Oak Hall on West Saanich Road.

The dedicated section, the second one for Anglicans, offered the promise of future business for the burial park, which was still facing keen competition from Ross Bay. In 1936, for example, 263 people had been buried at Ross Bay — the same number as in 1935. The cemetery by the sea was still showing no sign of filling up.

The cemetery trustees even asked Victoria city council to curtail interments in Ross Bay "for the benefit of Royal Oak." Oldfield was blunt. Royal Oak had been established, at a heavy financial commitment, as a replacement for Ross Bay, yet Ross Bay was still recording high numbers of interments. As a result, the situation at Royal Oak could not be supported.

Oldfield said that the board had reduced the price of plots at Royal Oak as far as possible in order to counter the effects of the financial depression. Graves in D Extension were going for $15 each, while those in the preferred sections were priced at $60 to $65.

The low-maintenance, plain-marker rule was still discouraging business. Royal Oak's marker requirements became a bit more flexible in June 1936, when bronze markers were approved. The move prompted a protest from stone cutters, concerned about the impact on their businesses.

The trustees considered getting rid of the burial park's team of horses in order to reduce expenditures. The next month they decided the horses could be put to work grading the roads in the burial park, and could be made available for hire to anyone in the district. That idea didn't stick. Two months later, it was decided to dispose of the horses after all.

The City of Victoria gave the cemetery a boost when it donated an old Ford delivery truck. With the licence plates removed, the truck was to be used only within the burial park.

A rumour that a new cemetery was being proposed for the area caused the board to note that competition would seriously affect the revenue of Royal Oak Burial Park. It argued that the cemeteries act should be amended to prevent this from happening.

The financial situation prompted the board to strip the superintendent of all spending authority. "No goods of any description shall be purchased for the burial park without having the order requisition verified either by the chairman or vice-chairman," the board ruled in October 1936. Also, it warned there might be a reduction in wages or in staff numbers.

John Wilkinson, the superintendent, died in 1937 after 14 years of service and was buried in Section D. He was succeeded by James Watt, one of the original maintenance employees. Watt and his wife moved into the superintendent's house, just inside the burial park's main entrance.

The superintendent's wife was a key part of the operation, although the salary paid to her – $10 a month in the 1930s – did not necessarily reflect her importance. She was expected to run the office, and to fill in for her husband when he was working on the cemetery grounds. The arrangement was not unusual at the time; in Spokane a few years earlier, Hiram Babcock's wife Gertrude had served in a similar fashion when they lived on the grounds of Riverside cemetery.

Watt became the top employee at a time when progress was finally being made on a long-standing goal – the establishment of the crematorium at the burial park. The idea had been discussed many times over the years. Cremation was commonplace in some countries, and was rising in popularity in others. In England, for example, laws were changed in the 1880s to make crematoriums possible.

In 1923, before Royal Oak was opened, the medical

health officer wrote to say that complaints had been received about "Hindu cremations at Ross Bay Cemetery," and that the Hindus might be willing to build a crematorium at the new cemetery if given permission to do so. The board agreed to this, as long as it had full control over the design and location of the building, and the Hindus paid the entire cost. (They meant Sikhs. At the time, the word Hindu – or Hindoo – was applied to anyone from the Indian subcontinent.)

In March 1924, the board approved the construction of a structure "to be used by the Hindoos for the cremation of their dead." The site chosen – the old quarry which had been the source of rocks for the roads in the park – would be leased for $1 a year, with a further charge for every cremation conducted. In July 1925, Bala Singh became the first person cremated on a wood-fuelled, open-air pyre at Royal Oak.

Several people argued for a regular indoor crematorium for the use of everyone. W. Cuthbert Holmes started the fight, and the Victoria Cremation Society pushed hard for a crematorium in 1927 and 1928. Eugene Sydney Woodward, a Victoria alderman, supported a crematorium at Ross Bay Cemetery, finally giving up the fight after two years in the face of opposition from the city solicitor, the parks committee, and about 200 residents of the Ross Bay area.

As a result, most of the bodies to be cremated were shipped to Seattle, with the ashes returned to Victoria a few days later to be buried, scattered or given to family members.

Little progress toward a crematorium was made until 1934, when the board secretary was asked to write to the city clerk in Vancouver for information on the status of a crematorium there. Victoria's engineer and building inspector were asked to prepare plans, and an application was made to the provincial secretary for health board approval.

In October, board chairman Oldfield and Victoria alderman John A. Worthington were authorized to go to Seattle or Tacoma to gather information for the proposed crematorium.

The Victoria and Saanich councils were asked the following month whether they would finance the construction of a crematorium. On December 6, Saanich council endorsed in principle a crematorium.

In March 1935, the board asked the councils to authorize and guarantee a loan of up to $12,500 to enable the board to proceed with a crematorium. A local businessman was prepared to lend the money as long as a guarantee was in place. At least two architects, Percy Fox and Charles Elwood Watkins, submitted plans for the crematorium and chapel.

The board favoured the Watkins design, but told him in September 1935 that his sketch plans were too "elaborate," and asked for modifications. Watkins removed a balcony, almost half the pews, and extra meeting rooms on either side of the main hallway, then submitted the revised plans.

The design called for a chapel in the Art Deco style popular at the time. Its smooth exterior walls would be punctuated by vertical projections, and the design would disguise the building's function. The interior would be finished in ivory with a golden oak lectern and benches of the same shade. Watkins said the chapel would hold 75 to 100 people.

In April 1936, the board approved the new concept, and told Watkins to proceed to working drawings. He completed them that fall. The crematorium was designed with one retort, or burning chamber, with a foundation for a second one included if demand warranted the addition.

With firm plans in place, the cemetery board still held

• The plan for a chapel and crematorium submitted by architect Percy Fox followed a more traditional style than the one selected.

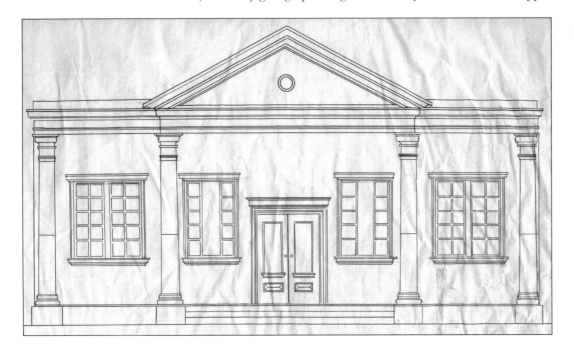

back. A crematorium was being built in Vancouver, and it was felt that the best strategy would be to wait to see what could be learned from the work being done across Georgia Strait. Finally, in early 1937, the proposal went back to the Victoria and Saanich councils.

Victoria council gave its unanimous approval on March 8, 1937, with alderman J.D. Hunter noting that the crematorium would be likely to help the cemetery get out of its perpetual deficits. Besides, he said, there was talk of private interests building a crematorium — something that would cause the city to face a considerable loss on its investment in the burial park.

The next day, despite the best efforts of members of the cemetery board, Saanich council rejected the crematorium proposal. Councillors wanted assurances that a Royal Oak crematorium would have a monopoly on the market in Greater Victoria. Two of the councillors protested that they had not been given enough information about what was planned. When it came to a vote, four councillors were opposed to the plan, and three were in favour.

The cemetery board tried again, promising to Saanich on April 13 that it would provide whatever information "any member of the council may desire." Two days later, Saanich council reversed its March decision, thanks in part to the absence of a councillor who had been against the idea the previous month. Reeve William Crouch cast the deciding vote, and the municipality was committed to backing the loan to build the crematorium.

Financing was in place thanks to the unidentified Victoria businessman who had agreed to provide $16,000. Twenty-year bonds, bearing interest of four per cent and payable semi-annually, would be issued to cover the loan. With money available, the cemetery board called for bids.

In June 1937, tenders for the crematorium project were opened. There were three, ranging from $17,400 to $18,696. (By comparison, at the time it was possible to buy a bungalow on an acre near Royal Oak for $2,650, or a two-storey home on the Gorge waterfront for $3,000.)

All three crematorium bids were deemed to be too high, so architect Watkins was told to talk to the low tenderer about possible alterations that could reduce the cost. On June 30, the

work was awarded to Luney Bros. Ltd., for $15,648, and the company started work on the project in early July. The building went up in record time. The first cremation, of May Willard from Sidney, took place on December 13, 1937.

The official opening of the crematorium took place on December 22, 1937. Victoria Mayor Andrew McGavin, Saanich Reeve William Crouch and members of both councils attended the event. Henry Clarence Oldfield, chairman of the Board of Cemetery Trustees of Greater Victoria, spoke on the history of cremation, and noted that the chapel would be used for regular funeral services as well as the ones preceding cremations.

The ceremony marked a turning point for the burial park. For the first time, it was offering a service that was unique on Vancouver Island.

• The interior of the Garden Chapel has remained basically unchanged since it opened.

• The Garden of Remembrance, seen here in the 1940s, is on the south side
of the Garden Chapel.

Evolution and expansion

Early 1938 saw the death of Margaretta Watson, who over several years had given so much to the burial park. The board of trustees provided a burial at no charge, placed a wreath on her grave, and sent a letter of sympathy to her family. It was a minor cost, given the hundreds of dollars that Watson had provided.

The burial park's financial problems continued for a few more years. It was unable to meet all of its obligations in 1938 and 1939, but with the arrival of the 1940s, Royal Oak became much more viable than before. It reported a small surplus by 1942, and in February 1946 it paid off the money it had borrowed from Saanich and Victoria, with cheques of $4,937.50 sent to each municipality.

The turnaround was triggered by the opening of the crematorium, which was in heavy demand right from the start. One local undertaker even asked for a price on cremating a man who had been buried at Ross Bay in 1894. Common sense prevailed, and the man was allowed to rest in peace.

The new facility was not without controversy. The board paid the Colonist to print 2,000 copies of a pamphlet, Cremation and the Bible, that it distributed to promote the concept of cremation. And leaders of the local Sikh community, which had been using the old rock quarry for its cremations, said the new crematorium was in conflict with their religion, so they would continue to use the outdoor one.

The opening of the crematorium prompted the establishment of a section exclusively for cremated remains. The spot chosen was south of the crematorium. Work on preparing the Garden of Remembrance began in May 1939, and local undertakers were invited to start using it in September. The following month, a sundial was ordered as an ornamental centrepiece for the section.

The burial park's financial squeeze continued for a few years after the crematorium opened, so management continued to watch every penny. In 1939, the burial park obtained a second-hand safe to keep its records, then bought a used truck for $95 to replace the one it had been given by the city. The old one was sold for $7.50.

James Watt, the superintendent, died of a heart attack in the cemetery office on January 3, 1939, after serving in the position for less than two years. The board voted to give one month's pay – $120 – to his wife, and provided a free grave. Watt was succeeded by Herbert Knight, a native of Sussex, England, who had been a cemetery employee since 1925.

The Second World War brought changes. Until June 1942, undertakers had driven family members to the burial park to make it easier for them to pick plots for their loved ones. That service ended when the federal government asked Canadians to reduce the use of tires.

The burial park set aside space for soldiers in the north end of Section B, an area developed in 1942. The section — the one closest to the entrance — features two distinctive retaining walls that were built at a cost of $575. The section was briefly known as The Terraces, a name brought back six decades later for another area with prominent retaining walls.

With the opening of Section B, the trustees introduced stricter rules on markers. Raised stones, even the relatively modest ones already used, would no longer be permitted. All new graves would have markers set flush with the ground.

The crematorium was kept busy and the board considered the possibility of doubling its capacity. It still did not have the support of the Sikh community, which continued to use the old quarry. The burial park trustees argued that outdoor cremations were a fire hazard, so the Sikh Khalsa Diwan Society asked for permission to build a small crematorium of their own. The request was denied, and the trustees said the Sikhs were "respectfully invited to use our crematory."

The 1946 annual report said the burial park's gross revenue was $47,149. There were 450 adult interments and 49 infant interments, with 186 plots sold and reserved. There were 233 cremations with 22 interment of ashes in regular sections and 45 in the Garden of Remembrance. New development had been started that would add three new sections to the north of the ones already in use — the area that had been rented to local farmers for a couple of decades. The triangle between Sections B, C and F was readied as well. It was called

• As the burial park expanded, more employees were hired and more equipment was purchased. This photograph was taken at the southern edge of Section F.

the Tri-Plot, but soon became known as the Triangle.

Charles Elwood Watkins, the architect who created the crematorium, died soon after it was opened. He was buried in Section C. Percy Fox, who had submitted a crematorium proposal that was not accepted, was buried in Section D. Many people in those years were opting for cremation – including Henry Esson Young, the medical health officer who approved the crematorium, Jennie and Robert Pim Butchart of Butchart Gardens fame, and former premier Thomas Dufferin Pattullo.

In 1949 the burial park's office was expanded. The $1,500 expenditure brought an addition measuring 12 feet by 25 feet, and plumbing as well. The change allowed the cemetery board to move its office there from Victoria City Hall.

In December 1951, all burial park employees were given a $50 bonus, and the board gave a box of candy to Lily Knight, the superintendent's wife.

Early the following year, the board considered bumping the hours of employees back by half an hour, to a start time of 8:30 a.m. rather than 8. That would allow funerals to be half an hour later, but the burial park's employees were not thrilled. Soon after that, they formed an employees' association, and by early 1953 the first working agreement was drafted.

Since it opened, the park had been home to wildlife, including rats, squirrels, rabbits, raccoons and deer. As the park became busier, the problems caused by those animals became more noticeable. In the 1950s, with more and more flowers being lost to the deer, Saanich council gave the park permission to shoot the culprits. Inspector George C. Stevenson of the provincial game department disagreed, saying it was wrong to harm them.

"They are deer from the Beaver-Elk Lake district and a few shots should scare them away," he said.

In the early 1950s, East Saanich Road was rebuilt into the Patricia Bay Highway, including a bypass around the Royal Oak commercial area. Traffic to and from downtown Victoria no longer had to go past the Saanich municipal hall at the corner of West Saanich and East Saanich roads. The bypass ran from the north end of Quadra Street to the burial park entrance.

A small stretch of East Saanich was turned into a frontage road to be used for access to the cemetery. The realignment meant the burial park's address became Patricia Bay Highway rather than East Saanich Road. It was still a simple matter to turn left onto the highway when leaving the park, or to walk across both lanes of the highway to catch a bus. The rush of traffic on the Pat Bay was still a few years away.

The size of the park itself was becoming an issue. Just three decades after it opened, and a decade and a half after the crematorium helped to put the burial park on a firm financial footing, the trustees could see that the park would soon run out of space. Saanich Reeve Joseph Casey predicted the burial park would use all of its suitable land within 15 years, so there was a clear need to acquire more.

One proposal that could have eased some of the pressure went nowhere. With the Chinese cemetery at Harling Point in Oak Bay getting close to capacity, the Chinese Consolidated Benevolent Association proposed to sell its land there to the municipality, and start a new cemetery adjacent to Royal Oak Burial Park.

The association approached Eric Elwell, a Saanich police officer who owned about 30 acres in two triangular parcels, one north of the burial park, and the other west of it, adjacent to the highway. The Elwell family had been farming the land, raising sheep and cattle as well as growing apples and loganberries. They sold some of their goods at a stand on East Saanich Road.

Elwell and the association could not come to terms. Elwell did not think that highway frontage was suitable for a cemetery, and was not eager to sell. Oak Bay council rejected the offer of the waterfront land. So the proposal faded away.

Another large parcel of land was just north of Elwell's property. The City of Victoria had owned the land since the 1800s, when it was acquired as part of the waterworks development at Elk and Beaver Lakes. The property had been used for the Elk Lake Game Farm for several years.

From 1910 to 1933, the provincial government raised pheasants for later release to hunters throughout British Columbia. In 1925, game farms in the Cedar Hill and Colquitz

areas were closed, with the operations consolidated at the Elk Lake Game Farm.

Under the direction of Joseph Jones, the Elk Lake farm had coops spread throughout a 30-acre site surrounded by a tall wire fence. Every year the farm raised about 3,000 birds and shipped them in boxes throughout Vancouver Island, the Lower Mainland, the Fraser Valley, and the Thompson and Okanagan regions in the Interior.

The farm lasted until the program was shut down in 1933. It had recorded two bad years, with a high number of unfertile eggs making the effort difficult to justify. The farm

• This 1950 photograph shows the provincial government's game farm north of the diagonal row of evergreens. The house on the game farm property is close to the site of the mausoleum.
Times Colonist

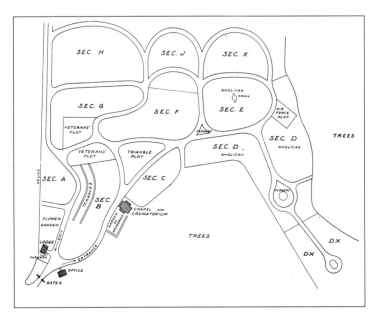

• A 1949 map reflected the early development of Royal Oak Burial Park.

was labour-intensive, with five employees needed to ensure that the hens were tending to the eggs and that rats were not eating the birds. After the farm closed, it was reported that the average cost of raising one pheasant for "liberation" was $45.29. Facing the severe economic depression of the 1930s, the province decided to give the pheasant-growing business to the private sector.

Jones moved to a new house across East Saanich Road from the game farm, which reverted to the city. The game farm property was rented to farmers in the area, including the Elwells, who needed land for grazing. Local police officers and gun clubs used it as a firing range.

In the 1950s, the house on the game farm land was dragged across the Elwell land to another property farther south. Other game farm buildings were falling into disrepair. It made sense that another use be found for the land, and with the burial park looking for more space, it seemed to be a logical fit.

The game farm was not the first choice of the cemetery trustees. They made tentative deals on two adjacent parcels, but pulled out of both agreements after deciding the land was not suitable. After that, the board told the City of Victoria that it wanted to talk about the game farm.

Just in time, too. In September 1955, Victoria Mayor Claude Harrison reported that only 13 plots were still available at Ross Bay. Royal Oak, he said, would surely see more activity as a result. He added that while there was a lot of space adjacent to the burial park for new development, a private company had approached the City of Victoria with a plan to develop a cemetery on the game farm land. That put pressure on the board to act.

The problem with buying the game farm was that it did not share a border with the burial park – Elwell's land was in the way. The cemetery board solved the problem in early 1956 by agreeing to spend $6,500 on Elwell's eastern 12 acres, the property directly north of the burial park. The deal allowed the Elwells to continue using the land until it was needed for cemetery purposes.

The Elwell land had been owned for a long time by Annandale Duncan Grieve, who had been buried a few years earlier in Section D at Royal Oak Burial Park.

Much of the Elwell land was too hilly and rocky to be used for burials, but the most important benefit for the cemetery was that it would gain direct access to the game farm. Now, it needed to reach a deal on the game farm land.

It took all that summer, in 1956, to hammer out the terms. Finally, in October, a tentative deal for 21.4 acres of the game farm property went to the city's finance committee, which recommended to council that it be accepted. The price was $18,000, and Mayor Percy Scurrah stressed that the cemetery board was getting a deal. A private party, he said, had offered $35,000 for the property.

The city retained the western part of the game farm, adjacent to the Patricia Bay Highway.

The cemetery expansion needed government approval, and it took two years to get it. The delay resulted from a proposal for a new cemetery in the Goldstream area. The cemetery board argued against the Goldstream proposal, and the company behind the Goldstream plan argued against the Royal Oak one.

In the end, after plenty of legal wrangling, Royal Oak was given the permission it needed to expand.

Royal Oak Burial Park wanted the land to meet future needs, not current ones, so it did nothing with its new property for more than a decade. It was not until 1966 that Section Q was created, pushing into the old Elwell property.

A more pressing concern was the capacity of its crematorium, which was dealing with increasing demand. That development was needed right away, not in the future. The board briefly considered erecting a new building, then decided to expand the existing one to the rear, leaving the front with the design Watkins had provided a couple of decades earlier. The expansion was completed in 1960 at a cost of $35,000.

New directions for the future

Herbert Knight, the superintendent since 1939, died on October 26, 1961. His death triggered significant changes in the operation of the burial park. The board dropped the title of superintendent and started referring to the top staff position as manager. In December, the new job was given to Leonard Treloar, who had been the board's secretary and assistant superintendent since 1949.

Knight's wife Lily had to move out of the house, but Treloar did not move in. The house went instead to the caretaker and his wife. With Lily Knight gone, the board authorized the hiring of a "female office assistant," and the telephone system was changed so the master control was in the office rather than the house. Now, the house phone would just be an extension of the one in the office.

There were other changes as well. The burial park started using walkie talkies so its employees could communicate more easily. It also put up a new equipment storage building for $17,000. The board was also hoping to replace its original office building — the one that dated back to Margaretta Watson's gift a quarter-century before. By 1967, tentative plans were prepared with an estimated cost of $20,000.

The big question, though, was where the office should go. The plan called for the building to be at the entrance of the burial park, next to the Patricia Bay Highway, which had become much busier with the opening of the provincial government's ferry terminal at Swartz Bay in 1960. That increased traffic raised the possibility that the highway would need to be widened, with the cemetery losing some of the real estate where it wanted to erect the building.

In June 1967, Victoria alderman Robert Baird, a ceme-

• Entrance gates in their original location next to East Saanich Road.

• The burial park's first office served for six decades.

tery trustee, went to the legislature for a scheduled meeting with Highways Minister Phil Gaglardi regarding his department's plans for the road. Gaglardi did not show, and the board was reduced to writing a letter to the department asking if any highway plans would affect the office proposal.

By late 1969, the highways department had confirmed that it needed land from the burial park entrance to widen the highway and to create Falaise Drive. The department covered the cost of moving the entrance gates back. The highway project gave the burial park a new address, its third — 4673 Falaise Drive, after being on East Saanich Road until the early 1950s, then Patricia Bay Highway. The project also meant that the burial park's plans for a new office were put on hold.

The cemetery trustees wanted more of the old game farm land, agreeing in 1970 to spend $50,000 on nine acres still owned by the city.

The same year, they agreed to a capital regional trail along the west side of the park. The trail was not built, but the cemetery property has still seen plenty of recreational use, thanks to a network of trails in the undeveloped areas as well

as the roads in the burial park itself.

The employees' association evolved into a formal union, with only one strike threatened in the first 20 years of its existence. That dispute was averted when the burial park agreed to pay its employees an extra five dollars a month. After that, salaries were tied to those negotiated by municipal workers in Victoria and Saanich. On the province-wide day of protest in 1983, the employees did not report to work, but burials and cremations had been postponed in advance of the announced stoppage.

The old superintendent's house, just inside the main gate, was used by resident caretaker William Jackson and his wife Dorothy until William died in the late 1970s. After that, the house was no longer used for official cemetery purposes, and was simply placed on the rental market.

In the late 1970s and early 1980s, the burial park negotiated a three-way land deal with the municipality of Saanich and the developers of the Broadmead subdivision, to the east of the burial park. Land that had been deemed unsuitable for cemetery purposes was given up for residential use. Parkland was dedicated along the burial park's eastern boundary.

In 1983, Roy Wootten, the chairman of the cemetery board, said that without more land the burial park would be full within 25 years. Another expansion was needed. The provincial government approved the addition of the last 17 acres that had been part of the old game farm. The land cost $205,000, with the expenditure split between the cemetery board, Saanich and Victoria. The highway redevelopment in the early 1970s had used some of the game farm land, but the property that remained could still provide plenty of room for the expansion of the burial park.

In June 1984, the Greater Victoria Council of Churches protested the condition of the crematorium chapel. The trustees replied that repairs were already planned. They also discussed converting the chapel into a columbarium, rather than restoring the interior. The following month, it was decided to leave the chapel as it was. By October, all of the repairs to the chapel, including roof plaster and paint, were completed. The ministerial association was advised of the work, and invited to visit.

After that, the cemetery board's building committee

looked at providing a new access so that bodies to be cremated would not have to be taken through the chapel. New double-doors on the north side, along with a small driveway, were approved and installed in 1986.

There were changes in the cemetery office. In August 1984, Ernest C. Bent was hired as assistant manager, effective October 1. He became manager on April 1, 1985, when Leonard Treloar retired.

An idea proposed by Hiram Babcock six decades earlier was revived in the 1980s. The board established a columbarium, an above-ground memorial spot for cremated remains. Fittingly, the first ashes placed in the Columbarium Grove were those of Arthur Ash, a former trustee and Saanich reeve who had been a champion of the columbarium project.

The opening of the Columbarium Grove in June 1988 marked the start of a new era at Royal Oak Burial Park. Other than the opening of the crematorium in 1937, the cemetery had been following the same basic model for almost 65 years. Now, the board started to offer more choices in ways to remember. It followed the Columbarium Grove with several new sections that reflected the changing tastes in memorial options.

In the 1980s, trustees twice turned down a chance to buy the former Caven land between the burial park and the highway. This land had been rejected at least five times over the decades. Finally, after it was subdivided, the cemetery board bought a small part of the Caven property, increasing its frontage on Falaise Drive adjacent to a private crematorium.

The burial park continued its unique relationship with its neighbours. In May 1988, the board paid $4,750 to have a paved pathway built between Royal Oak Drive and Falaise Drive, next to the Patricia Bay Highway on-ramp. That pathway provided better access for pedestrians visiting the burial park, as well as local residents going shopping or to school.

The area's park-like nature was recognized in another way in 1989. Saanich council rejected a proposal to develop five lots adjacent to the cemetery after residents said they had come to value the trees and the trails. Council decided to preserve the 4.14-hectare site rather than develop it.

In 1992, the cemetery trucked in fill to smooth out the valleys in the northern part of the park. Much of the fill came

from the Commonwealth Place construction site on Elk Lake Road. An access road into the burial park from Cherry Tree Bend was built to make the work easier, and to avoid the traffic congestion on Falaise Drive.

Change came in the office as well. Slowly. In 1986, trustees debated the wisdom of installing a computer in the office. That April, Ernest Bent, the manager, and trustee Bruce Ramsey went to Surrey to see a computer in use in a cemetery there. In March 1987, the trustees decided to get a new typewriter rather than a computer. The make and model of the typewriter were to be determined after a trial period.

In 1989 the notion of a computer was raised again, and the board decided to spend $1,000 to $1,200 on a study into the feasibility of a computer. In 1990, it was back to Surrey for another look at the computer there. The idea was then put on hold until 1992, when the trustees again debated the matter. That November, they decided that the burial park would get a computer system with accounting and word processing software. A database of historic records would come later.

• By the 1990s, when the Garden Chapel was added to Saanich's list of heritage buildings, it was almost obscured by trees.

• The mausoleum under construction in 1996.

Two months later, the board decided it would need to redo and rewire the office to make way for the computers. In May 1993, the matter was finally settled. Two computers would be purchased. With that, seven years of discussion about a computer came to an end.

In September 1991, the crematorium — built for $16,000 in 1937 and almost demolished in the late 1950s — was included on Saanich's list of heritage buildings. It was seen as a fine, rare example of the Art Deco style. Three years later, the burial park announced a $250,000 renovation of the crematorium. Much of the money was spent to improve the facility's environmental operating standards, with new cremation units replacing ones that had been in service for decades.

In late 1996, another part of Hiram Babcock's vision came into being with the opening of a mausoleum. The building provides above-ground interment spaces, and is designed as a place of peaceful reflection.

The following year, Bent retired as the cemetery's executive director. He was succeeded by Stephen Olson. Olson had been working for funeral homes for more than 20 years, and was the first manager at Royal Oak with experience in the industry. That reflected a major shift in thinking; seventy years earlier, a background in gardening had been considered the top requirement.

One of Olson's first projects was the restoration of the crematorium chapel, returning it to its original 1937 appearance. Watkins' remarkable design had been hidden over the years by trees and ivy, and many small alterations had been made with little regard for the integrity of the original design. The original entry doors, for example, had been removed, and metal-frame ones installed in their place. As part of the refurbishment, new wood-framed doors were crafted, with old photographs used as a guide to ensure that they matched the originals as closely as possible.

In 1998, the original office building, built in the 1930s with Margaretta Watson's money and expanded in the 1940s, was torn down. It was replaced with a much larger office.

The old superintendent's house was removed in 2002. It was briefly replaced with a small parking lot, then a Cross of Sacrifice that was erected by the Commonwealth War Graves Commission.

Other changes came in the burial areas, where there are more memorial options than ever before. As more people opt for cremation, it has become more important to find suitable memorials. These new choices at Royal Oak are designed to ensure that their names will live on.

It was already possible to dedicate rose bushes to loved ones; now, trees and benches could also be used to help remember them. Granite books, designed to bear the names of people who have been cremated, have been added.

A major shift in policy came in 2000 with the opening of Section W. The new section, north of the mausoleum, allows upright monuments, either standing on their own or as part of a feature rock wall. After years of requests, the public was finally able to place substantial monuments on graves at Royal Oak.

In 2002, the Memorial Woods nature path, north of the Columbarium Grove, was opened. It provides spaces for memorials set among plants native to Greater Victoria. There is room for the placement of cremated remains.

In 2008, the Terraces area, just north of the mausoleum,

was dedicated. It is the first area of the burial park to incorporate a water feature, 85 years after that lily pond was dumped from the original plan. The stepped design – similar to the look of some of the finest private estates in Europe and North America – helps to integrate the mausoleum building into the burial park's landscape.

The burial park also unveiled a "green burial" section on a hilltop at the north end of the cemetery. A person opting for a green burial isn't embalmed, nor will the grave have a concrete liner like the others at Royal Oak. Instead, bodies are wrapped in shrouds or clothing made from biodegradable material and put in biodegradable caskets.

The section will be left in a natural state, with no memorials or gravestones allowed. A common memorial at the entrance will list the people interred there. Trees and shrubs are permitted as a way of marking plots, and no pesticides are used in grounds maintenance.

The burial park has also opened a walking and cycling trail along its western boundary, adjacent to the Patricia Bay Highway. The trail, similar to one suggested several decades earlier, makes it easier for pedestrians and cyclists to get from Falaise Drive to the Cherry Tree Bend area without using the highway.

Royal Oak Burial Park's path to the future has been laid out in a master plan that specifies how it will be developed.

About 25 acres, where there are steep grades, rocks or fragile eco-systems, will remain untouched forever. Another 17 acres that have been cleared and graded will be developed as the land is needed. Wooded, level areas will be developed in small patches, preserving as many trees as possible.

The days of clear-cutting stands of trees and reshaping geography have come to an end; the new way is to integrate the cemetery's needs with its environment as much as possible. Today, the public treasures natural areas as parkland, while the original 1920s concept saw the park as something that needed to be created.

Despite the transformation, the original concept – the combination of parkland and cemetery – has been retained at Royal Oak Burial Park. It has become a landmark in Greater Victoria, helping to keep our history and memories close at hand.

• The Terraces, a section opened in 2008, is noted for its series of steps and a water feature, known as a rill.

Section by section

Royal Oak Burial Park is the final resting place for thousands of people. This part of the book includes information on people in most of the sections, as well as on some of those who have been cremated at Royal Oak. It provides a sense of the importance of Royal Oak in the history of Greater Victoria.

Each listing includes the person's name, date of death, and grave location, as well as co-ordinates that will make it easier to find plots. These co-ordinates can also be used as reference points in a search for graves nearby.

Location co-ordinates are not exact; there is a margin of error when using a Global Positioning System unit, and locations close to large trees are the toughest to pin down. These co-ordinates should, however, be accurate to within a few metres.

Most sections are identified by letter. Several sections – the Garden, the Grove and the Island of Remembrance, as well as the Columbarium Grove, the Memorial Woods and the Rose Garden – are for cremated remains exclusively.

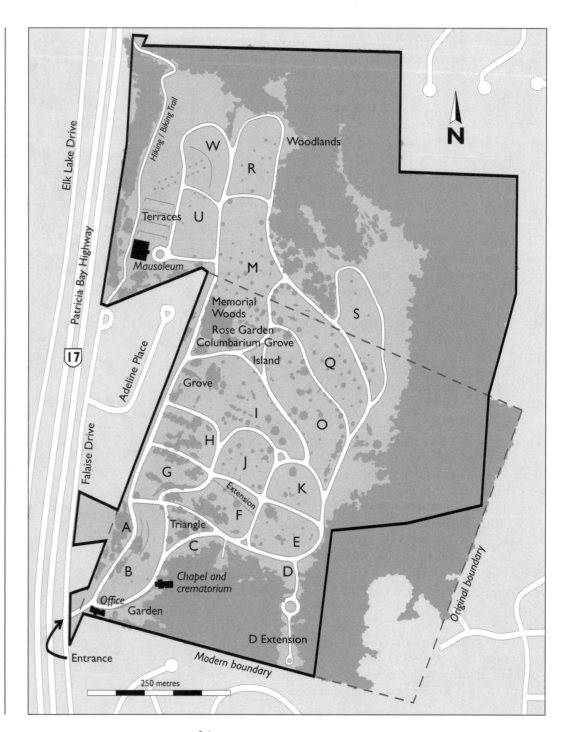

Section A

HIGGINS, Frank
Victoria lawyer, died September 21, 1953
A-015-26   48°30.199   123°23.026

Frank Higgins was a native of Victoria who practised law in the city for almost 60 years.

He was a son of David W. Higgins, a former editor of the Colonist and Speaker of the legislature, and Mary Jane Pidwell.

Before the establishment of Royal Oak Burial Park, Higgins was involved in the creation of a new cemetery in Vancouver. He also had a plan to open a private cemetery in Saanich. The proposal failed when the municipality refused to consider it.

JUSTICE, Anneta Margaret (Molly)
Murder victim, died January 18, 1943
A-007-03   48°30.183   123°23.011

Anneta Margaret (Molly) Justice was just 15 years old when she was stabbed to death in January 1943 beside the railway track near Swan Lake. The prime suspect was never charged.

The case was controversial because the suspect was related to the attorney-general. There were allegations of justice denied, and the suspect didn't help matters when he told police that he had committed the murder. Lingering suspicions resulted in a review of the case in the 1990s, after the death of the suspect. An examination of the facts determined that there had not been interference in the case.

• First used in 1938, this section is close to the burial park entrance, along the western boundary.

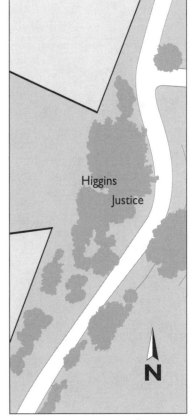

Section B

• Opened in 1942, this section is the first one seen on arrival at the burial park. It has two distinctive rock walls that gave it – briefly – the nickname Terraces.

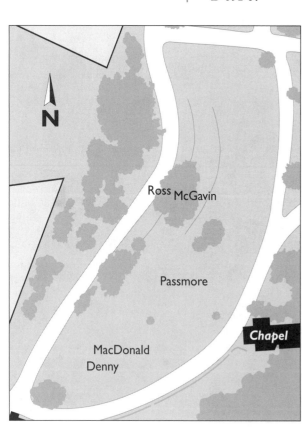

DENNY, Arthur Seckford
Furniture dealer, died October 8, 1945
B-091-09   48°30.152   123°23.029

Arthur Seckford Denny was one of the most influential businessmen in Victoria in the early 20th century. He founded Standard Furniture in 1912 and built it into a household name throughout the area. It was his second business venture; the first had been in New Westminster. When he died, the business was taken over by his sons, Thomas and Roy.

MacDONALD, Kenneth Cattanach
Provincial politician, died November 19, 1945
B-091-07   48°30.154   123°23.029

Kenneth Cattanach MacDonald was serving as British Columbia's minister of agriculture when he died.

He represented the North Okanagan in the legislative assembly for a total of 20 years.

MacDonald ran the agriculture ministry through a difficult time – the Great Depression. Agriculture was at a low level and marketing plans created great controversies.

During the Second World War, he led the drive for increased output.

McGAVIN, Andrew Ingram
Victoria mayor, died April 18, 1946
B-052-29
48°30.182   123°22.988

Andrew McGavin served as Victoria's mayor for eight years starting in 1937. He was born in Glasgow, Scotland, but came to Canada as a boy, settling in Portage la Prairie, Manitoba.

He arrived in Victoria in 1900, going into the wood-graining business, and started an automobile company in 1917. He joined the Victoria police commission in 1929 and was first elected to council in 1932.

The marker shows McGavin's name as MacGavin.

ROSS, Alexander
Alberta politician, died July 16, 1953
B-050-09   48°30.182   123°23.000

Alexander Ross was a stonemason. He came to Canada from Scotland in 1906.

Ross was elected to the Alberta legislature, representing Calgary Centre, as a Labour candidate in the 1917 election. He was re-elected in the 1921 election, which was won by the United Farmers of Alberta under Herbert Greenfield. The party had not run any candidates in Calgary, so Greenfield asked Ross to join his cabinet as minister of public works.

Ross won a by-election called to confirm his appointment to cabinet. He was defeated in an election five years later.

Ross was one of the founders of the Canadian Labour Party in 1922, and served on its executive with Elmer Roper, who is buried in Section E.

PASSMORE, Bruce Warren
Auto dealer, died June 19, 1994
B-073-10   48°30.162   123°23.001

Bruce Warren Passmore raced motorcycles and stock cars, flew his own plane and introduced the Volkswagen to Vancouver Island.

He started Speedway Volkswagen in 1951; it is the oldest established automobile dealership in Victoria.

Passmore worked in real estate, owned an automobile racetrack, the car dealership and also the now-closed Dingle House restaurant.

Section C

BRETHOUR, Samuel
Saanich pioneer, died June 6, 1941
C-101-E   48°30.166   123°22.939

Samuel Brethour lived in North Saanich for 68 of his 83 years, arriving from Ontario with his parents in 1873. The family became well-known in the farming community.

DIXON, John Hercules
Boer War veteran, died March 8, 1934
C-003-D   48°30.201   123°22.869

John Hercules Dixon was a native of Christchurch, New Zealand, but was raised in Auckland. He had military training at the Auckland Collegiate Institute.

He was one of the first Victorians to volunteer to fight in the South African war, and was wounded in action on February 18, 1900.

ELLIOTT, Percy Harris
College principal, died September 13, 1943
C-084-H   48°30.180   123°22.925

Percy Harris Elliott served as principal of Victoria College for 16 years, and ran the chemistry and physics departments at the same time.

He was also on the board of examiners of the provincial Department of Education for 25 years. He represented Victoria College on the senate of the University of British Columbia, where he had lectured for six years.

GOULD, Lauretta Bernard
Victoria pioneer, died May 9, 1936
C-086-D   48°30.172   123°22.936
GOULD, Isaac Archibald
Sealing mariner, died December 27, 1938
C-086-E   48°30.172   123°22.936

Lauretta Gould, who devoted her life to social work, pioneered a home for elderly women in Victoria. Born in Prince Edward Island, she lived in Victoria for 45 years.

Isaac Archibald Gould was a veteran of the local sealing industry. Born in Nova Scotia, Gould came to Victoria in 1891, and went sealing aboard the Ariel before becoming master of the Katherine and then the E.B. Marvin. He sailed to the Bering Strait and across to Japan.

After an international agreement ended sealing, Gould joined the staff at the William Head quarantine station, operating the tenders between shore and the ocean-going vessels. He also served as dockmaster of the Esquimalt docks.

MILLER, Thomas
Saskatchewan lieutenant-governor, died June 20, 1945
C-113-A   48°30.163   123°22.948

Thomas Miller worked as a newspaperman for 50 years. He was publisher of the Moose Jaw Times-Herald before he retired to Victoria. In February 1945, he was named lieutenant-

• This section is just north of the Garden Chapel. First used in 1933, it was the first section opened after the original ones that were developed in 1923.

• Section C, looking northwest toward the Triangle, in about 1948.

governor of Saskatchewan, but died in hospital in Regina just four months later. After a service in Regina, Miller's body was returned to Victoria for burial at Royal Oak.

PATRICK, Curtis Lester
Hockey legend, died June 1, 1960
C-073-C   48°30.176   123°22.928
PATRICK, Frank Alexis
Hockey legend, died June 29, 1960
C-073-E   48°30.179   123°22.923

Frank and Lester Patrick built artificial ice rinks in Victoria and Vancouver in 1911, and helped create the Pacific Coast Hockey League. They went on to become the most influential brother act the National Hockey League had ever seen.

Curtis Lester Patrick was involved in hockey for 50 years. He was a player and manager, and introduced the system of farm teams. He played on or managed 15 teams in Stanley Cup finals.

At age 44, he made a one-game comeback as a goaltender — he had been a defenceman in his playing days — when the regular goalie was injured. He allowed just one goal, and his New York Rangers beat the Montreal Maroons.

He was the driving force behind the Victoria Cougars, who won the Stanley Cup in 1925. In the 1950s, after he retired from the Rangers, he returned to Victoria and re-activated the Cougars.

Frank started his career in amateur ranks in Montreal in 1903, and ended it with his retirement in 1941 after he served as manager of the Montreal Canadiens for two years.

Frank helped shape the modern game. Among the innovations he brought to the game are the post-season playoff system, the forward pass, legalized puck kicking and the boarding penalty.

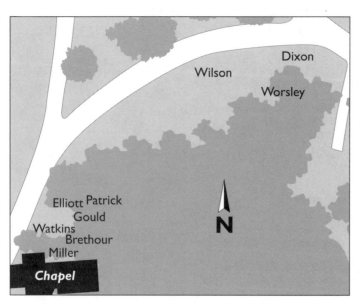

WATKINS, Charles Elwood
Victoria architect, died August 14, 1942
C-104-H   48°30.170   123°22.944

Charles Elwood Watkins was one of the most prominent architects in Victoria, responsible for Victoria High School, the nurses' homes at Royal Jubilee and St. Joseph's hospitals, Quadra, Oaklands, Willows, Monterey and Burnside schools, and the chapel at Royal Oak Burial Park.

He apprenticed to Thomas Hooper in 1890, and worked on the Metropolitan Church.

WILSON, David
Textbook officer, died May 15, 1935
C-035-B   48°30.194   123°22.903

David Wilson was born in New Brunswick and moved to British Columbia in 1884 to become principal of the Boys' School in New Westminster. In July 1887 he was appointed inspector of schools for British Columbia.

In July 1908 Wilson was named officer in charge of the textbook branch, a position he held until his retirement from the Department of Education in 1920. Wilson encouraged the development of school libraries by helping schools acquire the necessary books for their shelves.

Wilson was a Freemason. In 1896, he was appointed district deputy grand master of Victoria District, and in 1897 became district grand master. In 1898 he served a one-year term as the grand master.

WORSLEY, George Stanley
Police commissioner, died November 20, 1945
C-017-I   48°30.193   123°22.879

Col. George Stanley Worsley served with the Royal Artillery from 1885 to 1896, retiring with the rank of captain. He was appointed inspector of the Royal North West Mounted Police in 1901, superintendent in 1914 and assistant commissioner in 1922.

He commanded the Royal Canadian Mounted Police squadron sent to Siberia in 1918 as part of the Canadian Expeditionary Force. There, they helped the White Russians fight the Bolsheviks.

Section D (and extension)

BELL, Sir Charles Alfred
Indian administrator, died March 8, 1945
D-048-06   48°30.179   123°22.806

Sir Charles Alfred Bell, who retired to Victoria in 1939, served as the liaison officer between the British government and the theocratic state of Tibet and the Himalayan states of Sikkim and Bhutan. During an audience with the Dalai Lama, he became the only foreigner to sit on a level with the exalted Buddhist priest and ruler of Tibet.

Bell was born in India and was with the Indian Civil service. He had planned to write a book on the Dalai Lama while living in Victoria.

BURNETT, George Jennings
Organist and choirmaster, died January 10, 1941
D-016-10   48°30.180   123°22.746

George Jennings Burnett was considered to be one of the leading musicians in Victoria. He was prominent as an organist, choir leader, composer, teacher and organizer of concerts, both sacred and secular.

He served as the organist at the Calvary Baptist Church before moving to St. Andrew's Presbyterian Church as organist and choirmaster. From there he went to St. John's Church.

Burnett brought concert artists to Victoria and organized performances of Handel's Messiah in 1894 and Rossini's Stabat Mater in 1917.

He also served as choir director at Victoria High School. He wrote more than 100 anthems, chants and services, and piano, organ and orchestral works.

CROUCH, William
Saanich reeve, died July 12, 1953
D-E-G-039   48°30.097   123°22.760

William Crouch served as the reeve of Saanich for 12 years in the 1920s and 1930s, and became known as Mr. Saanich. He had entered local politics after moving to the area to retire in 1921.

He opposed plans to urbanize Saanich. He said that sidewalks and streetlights would make people soft. He preferred winding lanes, grassy slopes, and general stores at crossroads.

DAWSON, George Herbert
Surveyor-general, died March 26, 1940
D-088-05   48°30.155   123°22.746

George Herbert Dawson served as British Columbia's surveyor-general from 1910 to 1917, when timber licences made up the bulk of the work.

Before joining the government, Dawson had been one of Vancouver's best-known civil engineers in the 1890s. One of his biggest undertakings was laying out the townsite of North Vancouver.

DENISON, Francis Napier
Weather forecaster, died June 24, 1946
D-025-07   48°30.198   123°22.740

For years, Francis Napier Denison provided the daily weather forecasts for the Victoria region.

Denison was appointed weather forecaster and observer in Victoria in September 1898. He designed the Gonzales Observatory, considered at the time to be one of the finest in Canada. He served as its director from 1914 until his retirement in 1936.

He was well-known for his research into weather cycles and seismic disturbances. He presented papers to scientific conferences in England, Canada and the United States.

FETHERSTONHAUGH, William Samuel
Railway engineer, died April 17, 1947
D-026-12   48°30.200   123°22.730

Lt.-Col. William Samuel Fetherstonhaugh lived in Victoria for the last two years of his life. He was born in Ottawa, served in the First World War, and spent many years in Calgary working as an engineer for Canadian National Railways.

His son-in-law, Gerard Amerongen, was Speaker of the Alberta legislature in the Peter Lougheed government of the 1970s.

• Much of Section D was reserved by the Anglican Church for the use of its members. It also includes a military section.
The adjoining D Extension was designed as a low-cost alternative area, with no maintenance and no restriction on monuments. D and D Extension are the only sections in the park with roads through them. In this book, D-E and D-W indicate graves in the D Extension.

FOX, Percy
Victoria architect, died November 30, 1939
D-054-01   48°30.177   123°22.812

Percy Fox was an architect in Victoria for 28 years, first with Thomas Hooper and Son, and later in his own office. He designed several large blocks, including the Campbell Building, Spencer Building, Arcade Building and Dominion Hotel.

Fox also served as managing director of the Colwood and Willows Park thoroughbred race tracks, and was involved in the gold boom in the Zeballos region on the west coast of Vancouver Island.

HUGHES, Henry Thoresby
Monument engineer, died June 4, 1947
D-105-13   48°30.126   123°22.780

Brig.-Gen. Henry Thoresby Hughes was the chief engineer in the original construction of all the Canadian First World War monuments in Europe. Hughes spearheaded the search for appropriate sites, then oversaw construction of the monuments.

The Vimy Memorial in France was a subject of special pride for him. Hughes had been one of the first Royal Canadian Engineers and was posted to various places in Canada, including Work Point army base in Esquimalt. He returned to Victoria to retire.

LLOYD, George Exton
Church leader, Lloydminster, died December 8, 1940
D-083-12   48°30.151   123°22.777

Bishop George Exton Lloyd served in the Riel Rebellion, and later was named chaplain of the Isaac Barr colony. Lloyd's leadership role was recognized when the colony's main community was given the name Lloydminster.

He was made archdeacon of the Anglican church of Saskatchewan in 1907, and returned to England in 1917 to found the Fellowship of the Maple Leaf. In 1922 he was elected bishop of the diocese of Saskatchewan, and retained that position until retiring to Victoria in 1931.

Two of his sons, serving in Saskatchewan regiments, were killed in the First World War.

• In January 1945, flowers covered a grave in Section D.
Image 1984-017-003
courtesy of Saanich Archives

MAGRATH, Charles Alexander
Lethbridge pioneer, died October 30, 1949
D-060-16   48°30.165   123°22.776

Charles Alexander Magrath began his career as a land surveyor in the Northwest Territories.

In 1891 he became the first mayor of Lethbridge, Alberta, and was elected to the territorial legislature as well as the House of Commons in 1892. His name is found on Lethbridge's Mayor Magrath Drive as well as in the town of Magrath, south of Lethbridge.

Magrath was the chairman of a special commission that determined the routes of many of Ontario's highways. He served as chairman of the Hydro-Electric Power Commission of Ontario, and was Canada's fuel controller during the First World War.

He was the chairman of the Canadian section of the International Joint Commission. He retired to Victoria in 1937.

MANNING, Ernest Callaway
Chief forester, died February 6, 1941
D-093-38   48°30.144   123°22.770

Ernest Callaway Manning was the chief forester of British Columbia. Manning Provincial Park, between Hope and Princeton, was named in his honour.

Manning was born in Ontario, and graduated from the University of Toronto with a bachelor of science degree in forestry.

He was killed in Armstrong, Ontario, in the crash of a Trans-Canada Airways plane. He had been on loan to the federal government, but was hurrying home to Victoria to deliver a paper to a meeting of the Canadian Society of Forest Engineers.

MINOR, Charles Waldo
Cycling champion, died October 21, 1942
D-E-I-010   48°30.102   123°22.771

Charles Waldo Minor was a newcomer from Ontario, a watchmaker working for William Pennock and Alfred Clayton, in the spring of 1889.

Local bicycle enthusiasts had challenged a team from Washington state to a race around Beacon Hill Park on the Queen's Birthday, but when the Americans showed what they could do, the locals decided to forfeit the race.

Hearing this, Minor brought out his bicycle – a monster with a 54-inch wheel. He entered on behalf of Canada and his new home of Victoria.

He won the race and many new friends that day. He remained in Victoria until he died.

WATSON, James
Soccer player, died June 12, 1942
D-W-N-27   48°30.119   123°22.778

James Watson played professional football in Scotland for a team that travelled throughout the British Isles and Europe. He came to Canada in about 1920, when football – soccer – was all the rage on the West Coast.

He was the manager of the Nanaimo Wanderers in 1923, when they won the Connaught Cup, given each year to the top soccer team in the country.

After that, Watson worked in mills and as a janitor.

He lived in Powell River before he died on a visit to Victoria to see family.

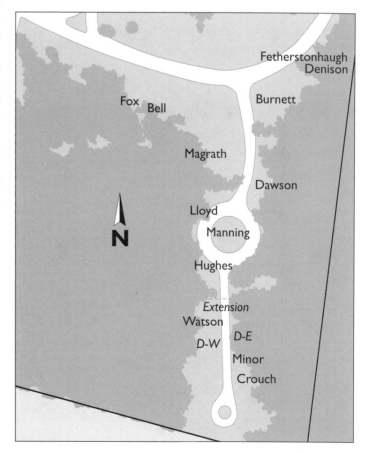

Section E

• One of the original three sections, first used in 1924. Soon after it was opened, it was reserved for the use of Anglicans.

AYLARD, George Henry
Mining pioneer, died April 16, 1932
E-061-I   48°30.203   123°22.796

George Henry Aylard was one of the leading figures in British Columbia's mining industry. Born in Palmyra, New York, in 1857, Aylard came to British Columbia in 1894.

He became manager of the Enterprise Mining Syndicate Company and the Slocan Mining Syndicate, both in Slocan, in 1895. He also took over the Standard Silver Lead Mining Company. He moved to Victoria in 1910 with his wife, Mary, and his children. Aylard was a member of the Union Club in Victoria and the Spokane City Club in Spokane.

BURKE-ROCHE, Edmund
Irish nobleman, died June 19, 1948
E-116-B   48°30.212   123°22.776

Edmund Burke-Roche was born in County Cork, Ireland, the son of the third Earl of Fermoy. In his youth he went to Wyoming to try his hand at ranching, and in 1898 came to Canada to become a prospector. He lived in Victoria for 40 years. Edmund was a brother of James Boothby Burke-Roche, one of Lady Diana Spencer's great-grandfathers.

CHAPMAN, John Howard Arthur
News photographer, died June 12, 1942
E-133-H   48°30.215   123°22.778

John Howard Arthur Chapman was a pioneer photographer responsible for many of the images in Victoria's newspapers in the 1920s and 1930s. He came to Victoria in 1890 and worked as a commercial salesman before becoming a photographer. He travelled extensively throughout the province with his camera. He took photographs for individuals and for businesses and also produced photos for postcards.

The British Columbia Archives has more than 3,000 Chapman photographs in its collection. Six of those photographs appear in this book.

DERMAN, Boris
Accident victim, died July 3, 1932
E-107-F   48°30.206   123°22.738

Boris Derman was just eight years old when he died, and the marker on his grave says "Forgive us dear son."

Boris lived with his family on Obed Avenue in Saanich. One summer day in 1932, Boris and three of his friends found a tin of dynamite detonators in an old barn near his house. Boris took the tin and threw it on the avenue's hard surface to try to open it. On his fourth try, the tin exploded, severely injuring him in the abdomen. He died within minutes.

The blast, which shook nearby houses, injured his three friends as well as three other people nearby. A coroner's jury determined that the death was accidental.

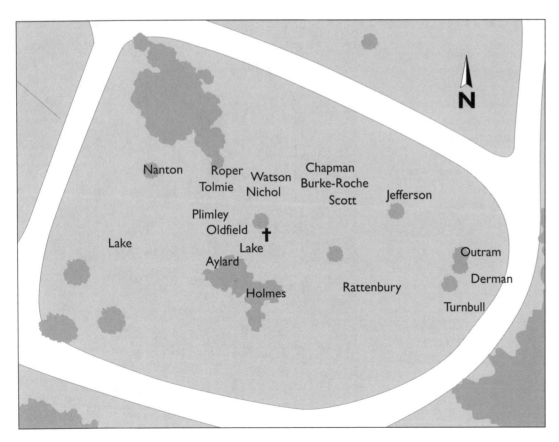

HOLMES, William Montague Hartley
Military, died January 1, 1925
E-062-B   48°30.198   123°22.789

Lieut. William Montague Hartley Holmes was serving with the Royal Canadian Artillery in Halifax when he was found in his room, shot dead. The medical examiner declared the shooting to be an accident, saying Holmes had been examining his rifle at the time.

Holmes was buried in Royal Oak with full military honours.

JEFFERSON, Robert
Poet and author, died August 7, 1934
E-146-H   48°30.215   123°22.760

Robert Jefferson was a pioneer resident of North Battleford, Saskatchewan, where he lived for 59 years. He worked as a provincial civil servant there, and was vice-president of the Saskatchewan Historical Society.

He recorded his impressions of early Saskatchewan in a book, Fifty Years in Saskatchewan, which was published by the provincial government. He also wrote poetry.

LAKE, Sir Percy
Military commander, died November 16, 1940
E-188-J   48°30.204   123°22.791
LAKE, Lady Hester
Died December 2, 1945
E-188-J   48°30.204   123°22.791

General Sir Percy Lake was a renowned military leader. He served as commander-in-chief of the Mesopotamian Expeditionary Force in the First World War, and grand president of the Royal Canadian Legion from 1934 to 1940.

He served for many years in India and Canada. He was quartermaster-general in Canada from 1893 to 1898, chief of the Canadian general staff from 1905 to 1908, and inspector-general from 1908 to 1910.

He won praise for the development of the Canadian forces, which made it possible to quickly pull together a full army with the start of the war in 1914.

Born in South Wales, Sir Percy retired from the military in 1919. He and his wife came to Victoria in 1923. Lady Hester Lake travelled with her husband in Ireland, India and Canada.

• The service for William Montague Hartley Holmes in January 1925.

Image I-68745 courtesy of Royal BC Museum, BC Archives

LAKE, Sir Richard Stuart
Saskatchewan lieutenant-governor, died April 23, 1950
E-053-G   48°30.207   123°22.822
LAKE, Lady Dorothy Marion S.
Died November 16, 1975
E-053-G   48°30.207   123°22.822

Sir Richard Stuart Lake served as the lieutenant-governor of Saskatchewan from 1915 to 1921. He settled in Saskatchewan in 1883 after working in the British civil service.

He and his wife were on the SS Athenia when it was torpedoed by a German submarine in 1939. They were rescued after spending nine hours in an open boat.

NANTON, Herbert Colbourne
Military officer, died May 1, 1935
E-121-F   48°30.220   123°22.801

Brigadier-General Herbert Colbourne Nanton was in charge of the mining operations at Vimy, France, which made possible the successful assault on the German-held ridge. Nanton retired to Victoria in 1928.

NICHOL, Walter Cameron
B.C. lieutenant-governor, died December 19, 1928
E-188-N   48°30.211   123°22.791

Walter Cameron Nichol founded the Province newspaper as a weekly in Victoria before moving it to Vancouver and expanding it to daily publication. He went on to become lieutenant-governor of British Columbia, serving from 1920 to 1926.

OLDFIELD, John Henry
Saanich pioneer, died October 16, 1924
E-083-A   48°30.210   123°22.795
OLDFIELD, Emma Louise
Saanich pioneer, died December 30, 1925
E-083-B   48°30.210   123°22.795

John Henry Oldfield came from Norfolk, England, by way of Jamaica and Winnipeg. In 1906 he bought 340 acres near Elk Lake sight unseen. John and his wife, Emma Louise — who was born in Ontario — came to Saanich in 1912, and built a house he named after his home back in England: Norfolk Lodge. The Oldfields were wealthy; John had a chauffeur to drive him around the community. Oldfield Road is named after the family.

OUTRAM, Sir James
Rocky Mountaineer, died March 12, 1925
E-141-J   48°30.205   123°22.738

Sir James Outram was a noted mountaineer who made twenty-eight first ascents of mountains in Banff National Park, including Cascade Mountain in 1900 and Mount Assiniboine the following year. His name lives on in the park. Mount Outram, above the confluence of the Howse and Glacier rivers, was named after him in 1920.

Outram, a clergyman, wrote the book In the Heart of the Canadian Rockies. He lived in Calgary, but died in Victoria while on vacation.

PLIMLEY, Thomas John
Automobile dealer, died December 18, 1929
E-084-G   48°30.211   123°22.804
PLIMLEY, Rhoda Harris
Automobile dealer, died September 21, 1927
E-084-F   48°30.211   123°22.804

The Plimleys founded one of the first auto dealerships in Victoria. Thomas John Plimley was trained as a manufacturing machinist, and worked for Albion Iron Works after coming to Victoria. He later began a bicycle business.

The Plimleys launched their first automobile dealership in 1905, and sold it a couple of years later. They started another in 1909 on Langley Street before moving to Johnson, Broughton, and then Yates, leading the move to an automobile strip on that street.

The Plimley name was associated with new-car sales in Victoria for almost three-quarters of a century.

RATTENBURY, Florence Eleanor
Architect's wife, died October 13, 1929
E-102-J   48°30.201   123°22.759

Florence Eleanor Rattenbury was the first wife of the famous architect who designed the B.C. Parliament Buildings, the Empress Hotel, the Crystal Pool and many other important buildings. She remained in Victoria when her husband moved with his new wife to England.

Francis Mawson Rattenbury was murdered in England after his new love found a new love of her own.

ROPER, Elmer Ernest
Alberta politician, died November 12, 1994
E-120-A   48°30.218   123°22.797
ROPER, Goldie
Died July 24, 1994
E-120-A   48°30.218   123°22.797

Elmer Ernest Roper was mayor of Edmonton from 1959 to 1963. It was his second career in politics; earlier, as the leader of the Co-operative Commonwealth Federation, he served 13 years as a member of the Alberta legislature.

Roper was born in Ingonish, Nova Scotia on June 4, 1893, the son of a sea captain. The family moved to Alberta in 1906. The following year, at age 14, he went to work as a printer. He met Goldie in Calgary and they married in June 1914. They moved to Edmonton in 1917 and Victoria in 1975.

The Ropers celebrated their 80th wedding anniversary a month before Goldie died.

SCOTT, Thomas Walter
Saskatchewan premier, died March 23, 1938
E-115-C   48°30.210   123°22.772

Newspaperman Thomas Walter Scott played a key role in the fight for autonomy for Alberta and Saskatchewan. Then he became the first premier of Saskatchewan.

He died in Guelph, Ontario after a long illness, but had been living in Victoria for the last 15 years of his life. His body was brought to Royal Oak Burial Park for burial. Today, his grave is one of the most visited ones in the cemetery.

TOLMIE, Simon Fraser
British Columbia premier, died October 13, 1937
E-120-J   48°30.217   123°22.798

Simon Fraser Tolmie was premier of British Columbia from 1928 to 1933. He was also elected as Victoria's member of Parliament five times, and served twice as the federal minister of agriculture.

Tolmie was the son of Dr. William Fraser Tolmie, a leading figure in Victoria's colonial times, and Jane (Wark) Tolmie, a daughter of a chief factor of the Hudson's Bay Company.

Trained as a veterinarian, Tolmie found work as an inspector of animals for the province and then the federal government. In 1917 he was invited to run for a seat in the House of Commons. He won and served there until 1928, when he was asked to take over the Conservative party in British Columbia. He carried the party to victory in a provincial election. The next year, the Depression started.

Tolmie's government was defeated in 1933, and Tolmie lost his own seat. Two years later, he was elected to Ottawa again, and died in office.

TURNBULL, Elizabeth
Sea rescue heroine, died April 30, 1968
E-105-H   48°30.200   123°22.745

Elizabeth Turnbull became a heroine in 1899, when she was still known as Elizabeth Annie Sea.

She was the assistant lighthouse keeper at the Berens Island Lighthouse, which once guarded the entrance to Victoria harbour. She spotted the sailboat Flora capsized beyond Ogden Point, and rowed out in a gale to rescue two men.

A year later, in almost identical circumstances, she rowed out to rescue the crew of a yacht which capsized in the Strait of Juan de Fuca.

WATSON, John
Business accountant, died January 22, 1931
E-188-K   48°30.214   123°22.790
WATSON, Margaretta Gray
Cemetery benefactor, died May 17, 1938
E-188-K   48°30.214   123°22.790

John Watson was employed by the Canadian Pacific Railway in Montreal and Nelson before working as an accountant for the Canadian Explosives Company in Victoria. After he was buried in Section E, his wife Margaretta gave more than $1,000 to the burial park for a variety of improvements.

• The cross at the centre of Section E has been a landmark since the 1920s.

Section F (and extension)

- One of the first sections, first used in 1923. F Extension, on the north side of F, was first used in 1948. In this book, F Extension graves are indicated by F-X.

ANGUS, Alexander
Bank manager, died July 17, 1927
F-029-C   48°30.210   123°22.850

ANGUS, Douglas Gilmore
Bank teller, died August 12, 1912
F-029-D   48°30.207   123°22.850

Douglas Gilmore Angus was working as a bank teller in Vernon when he suddenly took ill and died in 1912. His body was taken to Regina for burial.

Alexander Angus, his father, worked for the Bank of Montreal in Regina, and retired to Victoria in 1920.

In 1937, 25 years after he died, Douglas's body was exhumed from the cemetery in Regina and brought to Royal Oak. He was not buried in Royal Oak until 14 years after it opened, but of all the people in the burial park, he has been dead the longest.

GARESCHE, Arthur John
Victoria dentist, died September 13, 1952
F-X-013-03   48°30.231   123°22.836

When he died, Arthur John Garesche was the oldest and longest-practising dentist in Canada. He was 91 years old, and had been a dentist for 70 years. He had been working in Victoria since 1895.

He was born in California, and came to Victoria in 1866. He later worked in a railroad machine shop in Philadelphia before apprenticing as a dentist in Portland.

Garesche was also an enthusiastic amateur photographer, famous for his turn-of-the-century street scenes in Victoria, and was an early convert to the benefits of the horseless carriage.

HASTINGS, Thomas
Police chief, died August 5, 1927
F-071-J   48°30.245   123°22.882

Thomas Hastings served as the police chief in Saanich for almost three years.

He had served with the Edinburgh police in his native Scotland before coming to Canada in 1906.

Hastings was with the Victoria police force from 1907 to 1916, when he resigned to join the military police.

He joined the Saanich force in 1919 and became chief in 1924.

JONES, James William
Provincial politician, died May 2, 1954
F-150-F   48°30.226   123°22.850

James William Jones served for 17 years in the legislature. He was Speaker and later became minister of finance in the government of Simon Fraser Tolmie during the Depression years.

Born in Ontario, Jones came to British Columbia as a young man. He settled first in Kelowna, where he became a successful merchant and served as mayor from 1912 to 1917. He was first elected to the legislature in 1916.

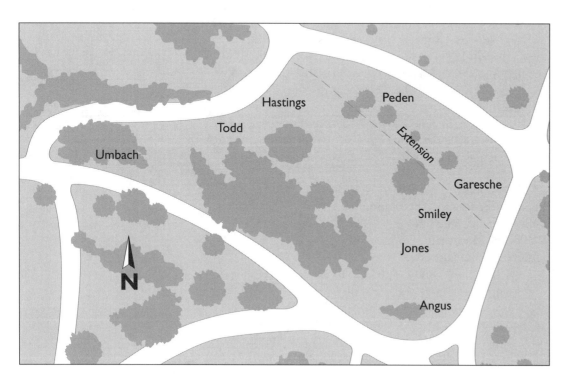

PEDEN, Doug
Sports legend, died April 11, 2005
F-X-009-07   **48°30.241**   **123°22.849**

Doug Peden is considered to be one of the greatest athletes British Columbia has ever seen. He was a charter member of both the Greater Victoria and B.C. sports halls of fame, and was inducted into the Canadian Sports Hall of Fame.

A member of the fabled Victoria Blue Ribbons and Dominoes national champion basketball dynasty, Peden was the leading scorer in pacing Canada to the silver medal at the 1936 Berlin Summer Olympics.

Peden went on to become a professional cyclist, a star of the six-day races that were all the rage in venues such as Maple Leaf Gardens and Madison Square Garden. He won seven major international races.

The Second World War meant Peden did not have a chance at a major-league baseball career. Rogers Hornsby recruited Peden to play baseball in the Pittsburgh Pirates chain in 1942 but that was interrupted by Peden's three years of overseas service with the Canadian forces.

Peden was sports editor of the Victoria Daily Times from 1953 to 1981.

SMILEY, Emma
Minister and teacher, died December 13, 1983
F-179-01   **48°30.232**   **123°22.846**

Rev. Emma Smiley, a doctor of divinity, gave weekly prayer meetings and Sunday sermons at the Victoria Truth Centre for more than 43 years. She served as vice-president of the International New Thought Alliance in the 1960s. She was a former teacher at the University of Metaphysics, Church of Truth in Spokane, Washington, and wrote three books.

She was brutally beaten by an assailant in her home. She died later in hospital.

TODD, Frederick Dundass
Photographer and apiarist, died April 20, 1926
F-067-E   **48°30.238**   **123°22.898**

Frederick Dundass Todd was the provincial apiarist until 1921. Born at Springfield, Fife, Scotland, on 30 April 1858, he trained as a teacher. After working as a teacher in Edinburgh, he moved to Chicago, where he was a photographic judge and publisher. In 1906 Todd moved to Medford, Oregon, and in 1910 made Victoria his home.

UMBACH, Joshua Edler
Surveyor-general, died February 2, 1930
F-058-E   **48°30.243**   **123°22.942**

Joshua Edler Umbach was named surveyor-general of British Columbia in 1916, and was working on the transfer of railway lands from the federal government at the time of his death.

Umbach devised a system of triangulation control surveys in an attempt to deal with the rugged terrain in much of the province.

He also completed a systematic survey of the areas that had been surveyed before his arrival in an attempt to bring more order to the work.

• The grave of William Anderson, who died in 1927.
Image I-68740 courtesy of Royal BC Museum, BC Archives

Triangle

• The Triangle was opened in 1946.

APNAUT, Julia
Cariboo pioneer, died November 6, 1952
Triangle 032-07 48°30.196   123°22.935

Julia Apnaut was born in New Westminster on March 17, 1861, the daughter of David and Mary Hamburger. Her mother had been born at Fort Langley in about 1844, and her father was a merchant, reportedly from Germany, with stores in Victoria, New Westminster and Barkerville.

When she was still a baby, Julia was taken to Barkerville over the old Cariboo Trail, riding in a basket on the back of her mother's pony.

Both of her parents died when she was quite young, so she was left in the care of the Sisters of St. Ann in Victoria. After a few years her mother's family took her to Maple Ridge, where she lived with the local First Nations, learning their language, customs and songs.

Many years later she recorded the songs for the British Columbia Archives.

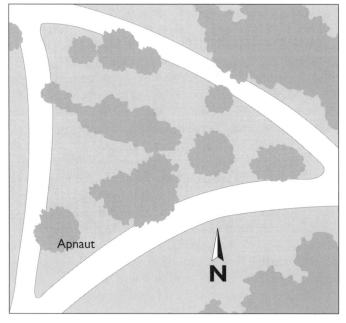

Apnaut

N

• An early view of the area that later became the Triangle.

Section G

ANDERSON, Elijah Howe
Pioneer, died July 9, 1928
G-213-H   48°30.262   123°22.937

Elijah Howe Anderson was a true pioneer of Victoria, having arrived in the city on the famous bride ship, the Tynemouth, in 1862. It was the first sail and steam packet to come to the port.

Anderson went to the Cariboo for the gold rush there, and farmed in the Cadboro Bay area. He also ran unsuccessfully for the school board as well as city council.

CAVEN, John
Saanich landowner, died March 9, 1949
G-003-01   48°30.254   123°22.989

Caven owned the land to the west of the burial park, including the property now used by the First Memorial crematorium. Caven was in the Imperial Army before coming to Victoria, and was captain in the Fifth Regiment here. He was secretary of the Uplands Golf Club for 15 years.

FYFE, Walter Colville
Military veteran, died December 13, 1946
G-038-B   48°30.247   123°22.977

Walter Colville Fyfe fought in the Northwest Rebellion of 1885, the Boer War and the First World War. Born in Quebec, he moved to Victoria in 1920.

GREENWOOD, Thomas Alfred
Klondike gold-seeker, died January 8, 1924
G-206-F   48°30.270   123°22.928

Thomas Greenwood was a pioneer of the Klondike gold rush and the Kootenay Lakes orchard country.

Greenwood came to western Canada in 1882, before the national railway was built. He went to the Klondike by way of Minneapolis and then the Edmonton trail.

Greenwood also served in France during the First World War.

JOHNS, Florence Mary
First person buried, died November 26, 1923
G-197-B   48°30.273   123°22.935

Florence Mary Johns was the first person buried in Royal Oak Burial Park. She died of cancer.

MYCOCK, Henry
Previous landowner, died November 13, 1927
G-260-H   48°30.268   123°22.914
MYCOCK, Rachel
Previous landowner, died October 1, 1930
G-260-G   48°30.269   123°22.914

Henry and Rachel Mycock arrived in Greater Victoria in 1888, and farmed for many years just east of East Saanich Road. They are buried on their old property — now known as Royal Oak Burial Park.

OLIVER, John
British Columbia premier, died August 17, 1927
G-195-E   48°30.270   123°22.943

John Oliver's headstone refers to the nickname — "Honest John" — that he earned as premier from 1918 to 1927. He was known for a high level of personal integrity.

He was first elected to the legislature in 1900, and sat for 10 consecutive sessions. He served as minister of agriculture and railways before becoming premier with the death of Premier Harlan Carey Brewster.

Oliver sponsored an irrigation program in the Okanagan Valley. The South Okanagan town of Oliver is named after him.

• One of the first sections, first used in 1923.

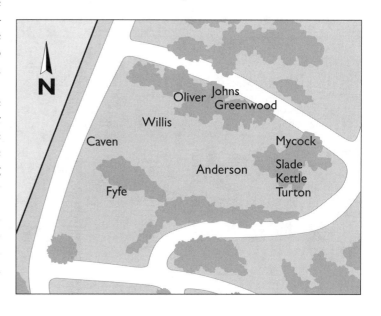

• This was all that was left of the car that carried Wilbert Kettle and Jack
Turton to their deaths in March 1929.

Image I-68744 courtesy of Royal BC Museum, BC Archives

SLADE, Ernest
Illness victim, died February 19, 1929
G-233-F   48°30.255   123°22.896

KETTLE, Wilbert
Accident victim, died March 11, 1929
G-233-G   48°30.255   123°22.896

TURTON, Jack
Accident victim, died March 10, 1929
G-233-M   48°30.255   123°22.896

One headstone bearing a Salvation Army crest has the names of three young friends interred close to each other.

Ernest Slade died in hospital of respiratory disease.

Three weeks later, a vehicle went out of control on Richmond Road and slammed into a telephone pole. Jack Turton was killed instantly, and Wilbert Kettle died a couple of hours later.

WILLIS, Samuel John
Pioneer educator, died April 23, 1947
G-176-F   48°30.268   123°22.950

Samuel John Willis was one of the architects of the educational structure in British Columbia. He was the first deputy minister of education, serving for 17 years until his retirement in 1945.

Willis was born in Prince Edward Island and educated at McGill University in Montreal. He came to British Columbia in about 1900 to teach, and worked as a teacher and principal on Vancouver Island and the Mainland.

He was also an associate professor at the University of British Columbia.

S.J. Willis School, which was opened in Victoria in 1950, is named after him.

• Section G before the shrubs grew into trees.

51

Section H

• On the hillside on the western boundary of the park. First used in 1948.

HORNER, Albert Edward
Saanich councillor, died October 18, 1967
H-076-16   48°30.311   123°22.946

Albert Edward Horner was elected to Saanich council in 1920, serving on the Victoria-Saanich parks board as well as the Board of Cemetery Trustees at the time that Royal Oak Burial Park was created.

Later, he was elected to the school board, and advocated the hiring of a school nurse. The Saanich board was reported to be the first in North America with a nurse.

Horner came to Canada from Yorkshire, England in 1875.

McCLUNG, Letitia Ellen (Nellie)
Author and activist, died September 1, 1951
H-063-17   48°30.297   123°22.917

Letitia Ellen (Nellie) McClung was well-known as a writer and a fighter for temperance and women's rights.

She campaigned for women's suffrage at the close of the First World War. She lectured across Canada and in 28 American states for two years before deciding to advance her cause through a seat in the provincial legislature.

She was elected in Edmonton in 1921, and held the seat for five years.

She was the first woman on the board of governors of the Canadian Broadcasting Corporation, serving from 1936 to 1942.

In 1938 she was a Canadian delegate to the League of Nations in Geneva.

After her family moved to the Gordon Head district of Saanich, McClung continued writing, and for a hobby grew prize onions.

She is best known, however, as one of the Famous Five women's leaders, who pursued the Persons Case to the British Privy Council in 1929. They established that women must be recognized as full persons under the law in Canada.

QUICK, William John
Saanich pioneer, died December 10, 1952
H-075-12   48°30.317   123°22.950

William Quick was the first Vancouver Island farmer to own a herd of purebred Jersey cows. His family, along with the Goyettes, Cheesemans and Rithets, played an important role in the incorporation of Saanich in 1906.

The Quicks lived on Wilkinson Road just west of Royal Oak. Quick's Bottom Park, on the north side of Wilkinson Road, is named for him.

WARREN, George Irving
Tourism promoter, died July 7, 1964
H-051-20   48°30.286   123°22.912

George Irving Warren was known as Mr. Victoria. He helped found the Victoria and Island Publicity Bureau and served as its head from 1921 to 1961.

Warren's efforts led to the creation of the Sidney-Anacortes ferry service, and he worked tirelessly to promote the slogan "Follow the birds to Victoria."

He believed that the city should retain its English feel, and deplored what he saw as a creeping Americanization of Victoria.

Warren was a native of San Francisco, and had lived there until he was 25.

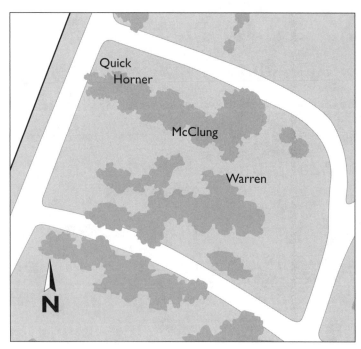

Section I

ARSENS, Lydia Augusta
Provincial politician, died February 25, 1983
I-159-19   48°30.315   123°22.801

Lydia Augusta Arsens was elected to the provincial legislature in the Social Credit victory of 1953, becoming the only female MLA in the house. Three years later, she was the only Socred defeated in the general election.

She blamed her loss on her outspoken views, primarily on health issues. She said, among other things, that doctors were ignoring a known cure for cancer, that fluoridation of water was bad, and that people were being poisoned by the food they eat. In the legislature, she argued against the consumption of coffee and tea. She also attacked candy shaped like cigarettes, cigars, and pipes.

BALL, John Thomas
Radio manufacturer, died August 28, 1968
I-095-10   48°30.316   123°22.856

John Thomas Ball produced hundreds of crystal and one-tube radios at his home on Harriet Road in the early 1920s, before many factory-made radios were available.

Ball opened the area's first electrical automotive business in 1920 and started making radio sets soon after. Demand took off after more radio signals were available in 1921.

Business slowed in the 1930s, but during the Second World War, when it was difficult to find factory radios, Ball again produced receivers for the eager public.

GENN, Reginald
Adventurous accountant, died May 7, 1953
I-086-15   48°30.327   123°22.896

Reginald Genn was educated in Liverpool, but ran away to west Africa when he was 14. A few years later he returned to England, then worked on two ships that went around Cape Horn to the Pacific Coast. On his second trip he deserted in San Francisco and made his way to Victoria, where his sister lived.

He tried a variety of business ventures, including a gold claim in the Yukon. He returned to Victoria, married, had a child, moved to New Zealand, returned to Victoria, moved to Scotland, returned to Victoria, and decided to stay. He got a job at an accounting firm and took it over in 1921.

HART, John
British Columbia premier, died April 7, 1957
I-149-08   48°30.325   123°22.838

John Hart served as premier of British Columbia from 1941 to 1947. He first ran for the legislature in 1916, and was elected as part of the Liberal sweep of the province. He was named minister of finance in 1917, and served until 1924 when he retired from politics.

In 1933 he ran for office again, and again became minister of finance. He retained that portfolio after he became premier in 1941. By the time he was finished, he had brought down 21 budgets.

• One of the largest sections, first used in 1953.

• A simple marker on the grave of a former premier, John Hart.

In 1949, he briefly served as Speaker before bowing out of public life. He never lost an election.

Hart created the B.C. Power Commission. He was also the driving force behind two major road projects — the highway between Prince George and Dawson Creek that bears his name, and the Hope-Princeton Highway.

LUM, Young Chow
Greenhouse operator, died April 11, 1956
I-029-17   48°30.310   123°22.891

Young Chow Lum was prominent in Saanich business for decades. Born in Sun Woi, Kwangtung, China, he was a resident of the Victoria area for 53 years. He started his first

greenhouse in the Fairfield area in 1921.

The crops grown in his greenhouses, established in 1924 north of Swan Lake, earned him the reputation as the Tomato King of Canada. His son Ed served as mayor of Saanich in the 1970s.

MAR, Art
Victoria merchant, died July 2, 1929
I-065-05-E   48°30.299   123°22.820

Art Mar was born in Canton, China, but lived in Victoria for 44 years. He was a well-known merchant and an agent for the American Mail Line of steamships.

He was first buried in the Chinese cemetery in 1929. His body was moved to Royal Oak Burial Park in 1971.

OWEN-FLOOD, Dermod
Supreme Court justice, died September 20, 2007
I-068-20   48°30.298   123°22.840

Dermod Owen-Flood practised law in Victoria from 1964 until 1987, when he was named a judge. He was appointed a justice of the B.C. Supreme Court in 1990 and remained on the bench until September 2006, when he turned 75 and was forced to retire.

Owen-Flood was born in Dublin and studied law at Trinity College in Dublin. He immigrated to Canada in 1956 and practised law in Edmonton and Banff before moving to Victoria. He was a professional actor while in college, and was known for the style and sense of drama he brought to his cases as a lawyer.

PARKER, Christine Mabel
Veteran's widow, died November 30, 1961
I-149-02   48°30.327   123°22.838

Christine Mabel (Newberry) Parker's husband Robert volunteered to serve in the First World War soon after fighting broke out. The Parkers had seven children and plans to build a new house near Quadra Street.

Robert was fatally injured in France. He is buried in Wimereux Cemetery, a few steps from "In Flanders Fields" poet John McCrae. Alone, Christine raised their seven children and ensured that Robert's dream house was built.

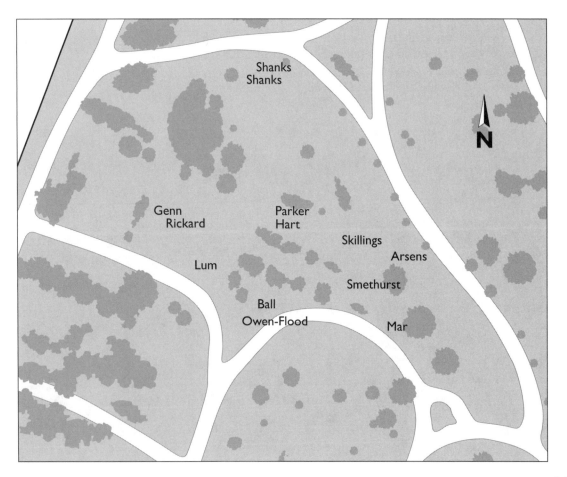

RICKARD, Thomas Arthur
Mining engineer, died August 15, 1953
I-085-07   48°30.325   123°22.899

Thomas Arthur Rickard was described in his obituary as stuffy, pedantic, bossy and intolerant. It was not all negative, though. Rickard had an extraordinary career, taking him from mining camps to the finest social circles.

He was a mining engineer by trade, and became the state geologist for Colorado and a lecturer on mining geology at Harvard. He was also editor of three mining magazines.

In his spare time, Rickard wrote books, including several on mining as well as a history of British Columbia. He retired to Victoria after living in England, Australia and the United States.

SHANKS, Reginald John
Motorcycle stunt rider, died January 16, 1999
I-223-20   48°30.364   123°22.842

Born in England, Reginald John Shanks came to Victoria as a child with his family. His father Richard opened a motorcycle shop on Fort Street, and after graduating from Victoria College, Shanks joined the business in 1928. He ran the shop until 1986, when he retired.

Shanks learned to drive a bike when he was 12 and was rarely off a machine after that. He became one of the West's best-known stunt riders. In addition to his biking, Shanks enjoyed his garden, was a gifted harmonica player and loved poetry. He is buried within steps of his father.

SHANKS, Richard
Motorcycle dealer, died March 26, 1963
I-215-20   48°30.357   123°22.852

Richard Shanks arrived in Victoria in 1912, and before long the name Shanks was synonymous with motorcycles.

Shanks served his apprenticeship in the trade of making and repairing pedal bicycles at the family shop in Chertsey, Surrey. He set up his own shop at Weybridge near the famous Brooklands car racing track. He changed the cycle shop into one of England's first garages. In 1907 he rode around Brooklands in a German Mercedes car with Dario Resta, the famous racing driver.

In 1911, Shanks sold his shop and moved to Canada. He managed a garage in Vancouver for about a year, then moved to Victoria to work in a garage. He soon opened a motorcycle shop and became the Harley-Davidson dealer.

He was a co-founder and charter member of Victoria Motorcycle Club in 1912. He was one of three men who rode motorcycles over the rugged Cariboo Trail before it was replaced by a highway.

SKILLINGS, Waldo McTavish
Provincial politician, died November 6, 1981
I-151-06   48°30.322   123°22.828

Waldo McTavish Skillings took over his father's firm, Victoria Baggage Company, and sought election as a Conservative in 1941.

In 1952 he switched to Social Credit, and won a seat in Victoria in 1960. He was re-elected three times.

He was appointed industrial development and trade and commerce minister in 1968.

Skillings lost his seat in 1972 when the New Democratic Party came to power.

SMETHURST, Henry
Boer War veteran,
died January 29, 1967
I-102-13
48°30.307   123°22.826

Henry Smethurst was one of 26 officers and men of the Fifth Regiment, Canadian Artillery, who left Victoria for South Africa on October 22, 1899. They were the first troops from Victoria to enter the Boer War.

Smethurst also fought in the First World War.

• The burial park takes on a festive appearance each December, when Christmas trees and decorations appear at or near graves.

Section J

• A small section on the lower hillside. First used in 1953.

GOYETTE, Joseph Henry
Saanich pioneer, died June 26, 1954
J-002-04   48°30.265   123°22.874

Joseph Henry Goyette was born in the Royal Oak area in 1878, the son of pioneers Joseph Goyette and his wife Cedra Cheeseman.

Both families had farms in the area; the Commonwealth Pool was built on the former Cheeseman property. The entrance of Royal Oak Burial Park is on land once owned by the Goyettes.

• In the late 1940s, the area that became Section J was not developed. It is just north of the F extension, new when this photograph was taken.

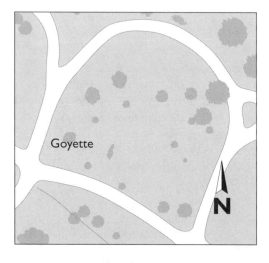

Goyette

N

Section K

A row of Catholic priests:
BUCKLEY, John Robert, died March 10, 1953
K-009-30   48°30.232   123°22.776
LESANN, Jean Pierre, died January 29, 1961
K-009-29   48°30.233   123°22.776
MANGAN, Thomas Joseph, died June 9, 1951
K-009-31   48°30.232   123°22.776
McKENZIE, Wilbert Basil, died May 16, 1966
K-009-26   48°30.234   123°22.774
McLELLAN, Alexander Joseph, died March 5, 1964
K-009-27   48°30.234   123°22.775
PENFOLD, John Henry, died November 1, 1962
K-009-28   48°30.233   123°22.775
WOOD, Anselm Bertie Walton, died July 11, 1949
K-009-32   48°30.231   123°22.776

Father John Robert Buckley, born in Halifax, served in the Diocese of Victoria for more than 40 years. For two decades he was pastor of Our Lady of Lourdes Church at the Willows.

Father Jean Pierre Lesann was born in Brittany, and was ordained to the priesthood in 1904. He was a missionary in Haiti until the start of the First World War, when he served in the French army. He was a priest at various locations in Saskatchewan before retiring to Victoria in 1945.

Rev. Thomas Joseph Mangan was a former pastor of Sacred Heart Church in the Lake Hill district. He also served in churches in Quebec City, Winnipeg, Toronto and Edmonton.

Monsignor Wilbert Basil McKenzie was pastor of Immaculate Conception church in Kelowna from 1931 to 1961. He also served in Salmon Arm, Revelstoke and Vancouver. He was ordained as a priest in 1919.

In Victoria, he was resident chaplain of the Mount St. Mary infirmary on Burdett Street until 1965.

Monsignor Alexander Joseph McLellan was chaplain of St. Joseph's Hospital for 25 years.

John Henry Penfold was pastor of the St. John the Baptist Church in Comox.

Monsignor Anselm Bertie Walton Wood served in the First World War as an army chaplain and in the Second World War as a navy chaplain. A native of Hertfordshire, England, he moved to Victoria in 1915. He was appointed rector of St. Andrew's Cathedral in 1921 and in 1925 was appointed pastor of St. Joseph's Church in Esquimalt, with the mission of St. Mary's in Victoria West. Later he merged the two churches to found the Church of Our Lady Queen of Peace on the Old Esquimalt Road.

LEACHMAN, Michael
"Hobo Mike," died September 1, 1981
K-033-19   48°30.246   123°22.798

Michael Leachman was a member of the Victoria Shrine Club and the Shrine Clown Unit.

His marker, which bears the nickname "Hobo Mike," reflects his enthusiasm for the cause.

WYLIE, Edmund Richard
Saskatchewan judge, died October 7, 1951
K-044-12   48°30.255   123°22.767

Edmund Richard Wylie was a judge in the Estevan judicial district in Saskatchewan. Born in Ontario, he taught school in Saskatchewan before articling as a lawyer.

He was the Moosomin town solicitor from 1907 to 1914, and served on several education and community boards.

He also sat on the council of district court judges and the council of surrogate court judges, served on the 1931 royal commission into the lignite coal strike, and was a member of several provincial commissions.

Wylie moved to Victoria in 1948 after retiring from the Saskatchewan bench.

• First used in 1948. Much of it was reserved for members of the Catholic church.

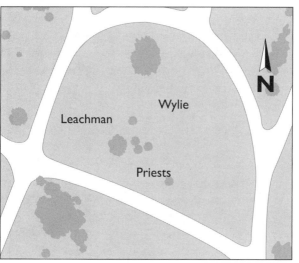

Section M

• This section was opened in two pieces – the southern half in 1959, and the northern half in 1978 after the cemetery's boundaries had been expanded.

ANDERSEN, Henry Christian
Canadian Pacific ferries, died June 3, 1983
M-132-25   48°30.459   123°22.877

Henry Christian Andersen was born in Tonsberg, Norway in 1889, and died in Vancouver. He was a pioneer master mariner for the coastal routes run by Canadian Pacific Steamships.

His son Robert, buried next to him, was a captain for B.C. Ferries.

ANDERSEN, Robert Henry
B.C. Ferries, died January 21, 2007
M-132-23   48°30.460   123°22.876

Capt. Robert Henry Andersen joined the Royal Canadian Navy at age 17 and served in the Second World War in the Atlantic. He worked for B.C Coast Steamships from 1945 to 1963, when he joined B.C. Ferries.

He became a master in 1968 on the Saltspring-Tsawwassen route. In 1976 he moved to Victoria to finish his career on the Swartz Bay-Tsawwassen route.

ELWELL, Eric Charles
Policeman and farmer,
died February 27, 1962
M-066-03E
48°30.406   123°22.832

Eric Charles Elwell, right, worked as a policeman in Saanich from 1930 to 1954. He was also a farmer, raising sheep and cattle and growing fruit on land adjacent to Royal Oak Burial Park in the 1950s.

When the cemetery board looked to expand its property, Elwell agreed to sell. The Elwells continued to use the land until it was needed by the burial park.

The Elwell land has been incorporated into the burial park, and is no longer identifiable. It includes much of section S and the north portions of M and Q.

Photograph courtesy Ben Elwell

CABELDU, Frederick Norman
Military, died June 12, 1976
M-085-12   48°30.420   123°22.836

Frederick Norman Cabeldu led Victoria's Canadian Scottish Regiment in the D-Day landing in June 1944, and saw further action that gained him several decorations.

He joined the militia in 1926, had risen to major by 1937 and went overseas as company commander. He became second in command in 1943, and lieutenant-colonel soon after. He was the only person from Victoria with advance knowledge of the details of the Allied invasion.

He also served on Victoria city council and as head of his real estate company. He was president of the Union Club and the Victoria Real Estate Board.

MYCOCK, Jesse
Original resident, died July 29, 1963
M-069-11   48°30.403   123°22.820
MYCOCK, Gladys
Original resident, died May 8, 1967
M-069-12   48°30.404   123°22.820

Both Gladys and Jesse Mycock were buried on land previously owned by their families. Jesse was a son of Henry and Rachel, who had sold the land to the cemetery board in 1922. Gladys was born a Heal – and the Heals had owned the cemetery land before selling it to the Mycocks.

RYAN, Joseph (Joe)
Football manager, died June 2, 1979
M-183-05   48°30.475   123°22.824

Joseph (Joe) Ryan was a founder of the Winnipeg Blue Bombers and a member of the Canadian Football Hall of Fame. He also helped start two other teams, the Montreal Alouettes and the Edmonton Eskimos.

A sports columnist in Winnipeg before getting involved in team management, Ryan was the first Canadian Football League manager to import players directly from the United States.

He retired from football in 1963 and moved to Victoria.

SAMPSON, Arthur Joseph
War veteran, died August 11, 1995
M-164-33   48°30.454   123°22.846

Arthur Sampson was one of the first Canadian soldiers to go ashore in the battle to liberate Sicily in the Second World War. He was captured by the Germans and sent to a prisoner-of-war camp, Stalag VIIA, in mainland Italy.

As the Allies pushed, the Germans retreated, and Sampson had to go on some forced marches to other camps. During one of the marches, Sampson and two other men ran away. One of the other men was shot and killed.

Sampson hid on a farm in Italy for several months until the area was liberated and it was safe to come out.

STRAITH, William Thomas
Provincial politician, died March 27, 1980
M-059-16   48°30.400   123°22.851

William Thomas Straith was elected to the provincial legislature as a Liberal in 1937. Ten years later, he was named education minister in the coalition government. As education minister, he travelled about 40,000 kilometres a year.

In 1951 he was named provincial secretary, but left politics when Social Credit swept the province the following year.

Before and after his political life, Straith was a lawyer in Victoria.

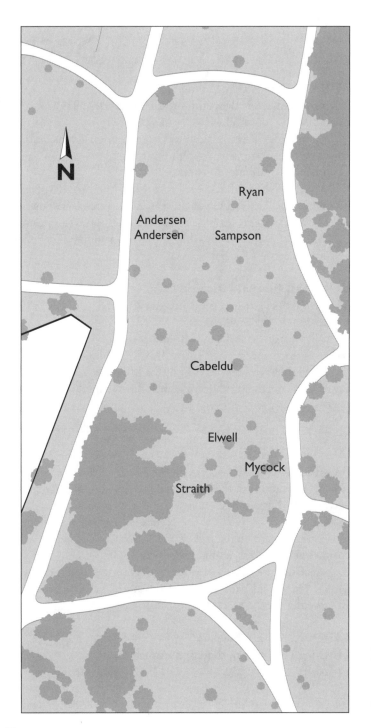

Section O

• Opened in 1957, this section came close to the northern boundary of the original burial park property.

AUDAIN, James Guy Payne
Author, Dunsmuir descendant, died October 30, 1970
O-160-04   48°30.341   123°22.777

James Guy Payne Audain was a grandson of James Dunsmuir, British Columbia's 14th premier, and a great-grandson of industrialist Robert Dunsmuir.

Audain wrote the book From Coal Mine to Castle, a biography of Robert Dunsmuir, as well as Alex Dunsmuir's Dilemma, which was about his great-uncle's business interests.

Audain also tried his hand at politics, running federally and for a seat on Oak Bay council.

BOURKE, Rowland Richard Louis
Victoria Cross winner, died August 29, 1958
O-010-16   48°30.261   123°22.739

Rowland Richard Louis Bourke was awarded the Victoria Cross for his actions at Ostend, Belgium during the First World War. He was a lieutenant in the Royal Naval Volunteer Reserve, commanding a motor launch that went into Ostend's harbour to ensure that everyone had been safely taken off the HMS Vindictive.

He rescued an officer and two seamen he found clinging to an overturned boat. His motor launch came under heavy fire and was hit 55 times, once by a six-inch shell which killed two of her crew and did considerable damage. Bourke managed to take her into the open sea, and was taken in tow.

The Victoria Cross is the highest and most prestigious award for gallantry in the face of the enemy that can be awarded to British and Commonwealth forces.

Bourke was also awarded the Distinguished Service Order. He served with the Royal Canadian Naval Volunteer Reserve during the Second World War.

CHANT, William Neelands
Provincial politician, died September 25, 1976
O-180-03   48°30.347   123°22.750

William Neelands Chant was the only person to hold cabinet portfolios under William Aberhart in Alberta and W.A.C. Bennett in British Columbia.

Chant became a member of Aberhart's first cabinet in 1935, serving as agriculture minister. Aberhart fired him in 1937, apparently because Chant had refused to dismiss key officials.

He moved to Victoria in 1948 and was elected to represent Victoria in 1953. Chant became public works minister, and held the post until he retired in 1972.

FIRESTONE, Otto Jack
Ottawa businessman, died October 14, 1993
O-009-7   48°30.259   123°22.743

Otto Jack Firestone was a former senior public servant, special adviser to legendary cabinet minister C.D. Howe, an economist, academic and scholar.

He also dabbled in real estate and other investments to build Terrace Investments and Capro Investments into multi-million-dollar holding companies during the 1950s and 1960s.

He amassed one of the largest Canadian art collections assembled by a private collector, containing more than 1,500 works by 200 different artists.

Firestone lived in Victoria for about a year before his death. His son Bruce was instrumental in bringing the National Hockey League back to Ottawa.

MAYHEW, Robert Wellington
Businessman and politician, died July 28, 1971
O-182-17   48°30.343   123°22.747

Robert Wellington Mayhew built a successful roofing business with 400 people on the payroll when he sold it in 1957. His real success came, however, in politics.

Mayhew was on Oak Bay council from 1932 to 1936. In 1937 he was elected Victoria's member of Parliament and held the seat until 1952.

He served as finance minister and fisheries minister in Liberal governments.

After serving in Ottawa, Mayhew was named Canada's ambassador to Japan.

McGILL, William Weir
Victoria pharmacist, died March 13, 1994
O-198-04   48°30.361   123°22.793

William Weir (Mac) McGill was a pharmacist for 80 years and a founder of McGill and Orme pharmacy.

Born in Guelph, Ontario, McGill studied at the Ontario College of Pharmacy, moved west in 1912, served as a flyer in the First World War, worked in a Vancouver drugstore and met Cyril Orme.

On November 7, 1930 the first McGill and Orme opened in the Castle Building on Broad and Fort streets. McGill sold his share in 1945, but continued to work there until 1990.

ORME, Cyril Hodgins
Victoria pharmacist, died August 17, 1961
O-221-06   48°30.370   123°22.766

Cyril Hodgins Orme was one of the founders of McGill and Orme, one of the best-known pharmacy companies in Victoria.

He was also the founder of Orme Prescriptions, which operated from 1955 through 1958.

SLOAN, Gordon McGregor
Chief justice, died January 14, 1959
O-239-07   48°30.377   123°22.766

The day Gordon McGregor Sloan died, the Victoria Times said in an editorial that he had "unquestionably influenced the future of British Columbia more than any other man of his generation."

Sloan was born in Nanaimo, the son of William Sloan, who served in the provincial cabinet. Gordon Sloan served as a pilot in the First World War, then studied law on his return to Canada.

He was called to the bar in 1921.

He was elected to the provincial government in 1933, and was named attorney general – at 35, the youngest in the history of the province.

In 1942, Sloan left politics to serve on the Court of Appeal, and became Chief Justice in 1944. He presided over some of the most important royal commissions of his era,

dealing with salmon fisheries, the forest industry and workers' compensation.

Sloan served as a mediator in major labour disputes and was the official administrator when the lieutenant-governor was out of Victoria.

The year before he died, he left the court to become the British Columbia government's top adviser on forestry issues.

THOMAS, John Morris
Federal politician,
died December 10, 1962
O-151-12
48°30.331   123°22.738

John Morris Thomas helped found the Co-operative Commonwealth Federation and helped with Major James Coldwell's first political campaign. He was the party's candidate in Esquimalt-Saanich in three federal elections.

Thomas farmed on the Prairies in the 1920s, and then was a school principal on Vancouver Island until he retired in 1956.

TOONE, Alfred Walter
Victoria mayor,
died November 15, 1966
O-135-20
48°30.321   123°22.746

Alfred Walter Toone served on Victoria council for five years, and as mayor for 11 months, until he died in office.

He ran a photographic business before the Second World War, then went overseas with the Canadian army. On his return he worked in local shipyards, and became president of his union as well as the Meal Trades Council.

He was secretary-treasurer of the Victoria Labour Council when he was elected mayor.

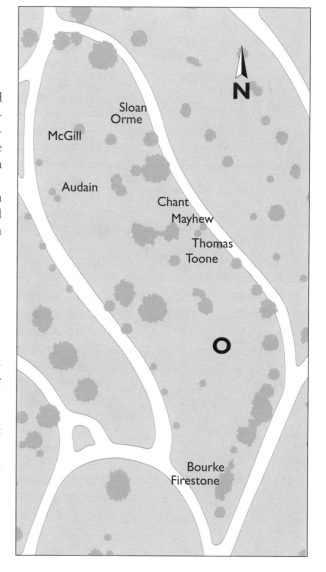

Section Q

• One of the largest sections, opened in 1966.

BITTERMAN family
Accident victims, died June 5, 1968
Q-034-18   48°30.353   123°22.735

Four of the five members of the Bitterman family were killed in a landslide near Revelstoke. Parents Ernest John and Annet Bitterman died, along with daughters Terri Lynn, four, and Sandra Lee, two. A six-year-old daughter survived.

The Bittermans had been returning from a vacation in Saskatchewan. The landslide pushed the Bitterman car down a 150-foot embankment. It ended up 250 feet from the highway. The landslide forced the closure of the Trans-Canada Highway for two days.

DAMUDE, Darin Jon
Murder victim, died March 19, 1995
Q-092-24   48°30.384   123°22.708
DAMUDE, Sheila Mae
Murder victim, died March 19, 1995
Q-092-24   48°30.384   123°22.709

Sheila Mae Damude worked on election campaigns for former Victoria Mayor Bob Cross and for Hugh Curtis, former B.C. finance minister and Social Credit MLA for Saanich and the Islands.

Sheila and her son Darin were murdered in Thailand. Sheila had gone there for a rendezvous with Darin, who had spent two months travelling in India and Southeast Asia. The prime suspect in the murders, an escaped convict from England, was hanged in Singapore for the killing of a South African tourist. He was never charged in the Damude murders.

JAMES, Percy Leonard
Victoria architect, died January 3, 1970
Q-068-06   48°30.382   123°22.763

Percy Leonard James was responsible for the design of many of the most prominent buildings in Greater Victoria. He was associated with Francis Mawson Rattenbury in 1924 and 1925, and together they created plans for the Canadian Pacific terminal and the Crystal Garden.

That work led to another commission for James – the swimming pool at the Canadian Pacific hotel at Lake Louise, Alberta.

Working with his brother Douglas, James compiled an impressive resume of buildings in Oak Bay and Victoria, including private houses, the Oak Bay municipal hall, St. Mary's Anglican Church, and the federal building erected at the end of the Second World War.

His portfolio also included the east wing of the Royal Jubilee Hospital, two clubhouses at the old Royal Colwood Golf Club – the first was destroyed by fire – as well as Oak Bay Junior Secondary School.

Working with J.C.M. Keith, James won the competition for the original Essondale hospital, but the work was not carried out.

KEATS, Gordon Blanchard (Duke)
Hockey player, died January 16, 1972
Q-089-03   48°30.389   123°22.717

Gordon Blanchard (Duke) Keats grew up in North Bay, Ontario, and started playing hockey as a young boy. In 1915 he joined the Toronto Blueshirts of the National Hockey Association, finishing fifth in league scoring with 22 goals in 24 games.

After serving in the First World War, Keats moved west, playing for the Edmonton Eskimos of the Western Canada Hockey League. That league folded in 1926. Keats played with Boston, Detroit and Chicago in the National Hockey League over the next three years.

After a couple of years in the American Hockey Association, Keats returned to Edmonton and the Eskimos, by that time playing in the North West Hockey League. Keats was inducted into the Hockey Hall of Fame in 1958.

MacDONALD, John
Gasoline retailer, died April 19, 1970
Q-053-27   48°30.363   123°22.691

John MacDonald started a drive-in pump gas station in

Victoria in 1914, one of the first in North America. MacDonald's Imperial Oil station was on the northwest corner of Douglas and Broughton streets.

Equipment included a one-gallon hand-operated pump, underground storage tanks, bulk motor oil served "on tap," a rest room and free air and water. Gasoline was 16 cents a gallon, and oil 30 cents a quart.

MARTIN, Eric Charles Fitzgerald
Provincial politician, died April 23, 1973
Q-088-33   48°30.383   123°22.730

Eric Charles Fitzgerald Martin was an original member of W.A.C. Bennett's cabinet in 1952. He was a controversial minister of health, and resigned in 1966 after producing a doctor's report showing that he was suffering from a lung ailment caused by heavy smoking.

He was not trying to caution people against smoking — he was trying to prove that he was not being forced from the cabinet.

The Eric Martin Pavilion at Royal Jubilee Hospital was named after him.

McMORRAN, George Stark
Cordova Bay pioneer, died April 23, 1971
Q-106-12   48°30.400   123°22.733

George Stark McMorran was just one year old when he first saw Cordova Bay. His father had brought the family to Saanich from Ontario so he could take a job as manager of the Rithet farm, and the McMorrans camped on the beach until they found better lodgings.

McMorran served in the First World War. On May 24, 1919, he opened a tea room above the beach at Cordova Bay. Soon after, he added a general store, and in 1926 was named the postmaster. An auto camp came later.

The auto camp, store and post office are long gone, but the McMorran property has evolved into a Cordova Bay institution — McMorran's restaurant and dance hall.

WALLS, Warren
Motorcycle wizard, died January 1, 1976
Q-122-38   48°30.426   123°22.800

Warren Walls was a fixture in Victoria's motorcycle scene, known for his ability to build custom choppers that were among the best on the West Coast.

He died after binge drinking at a party on January 1, 1976, just 28 years old.

Every New Year's Day, a procession of motorcycles heads to Walls' grave, which is marked with an elaborate stone featuring a motorcycle and this inscription: "Bounty Hunter forever."

WATSON, James Curtis
First World War pilot,
died September 25, 1971
Q-086-07
48°30.388   123°22.733
WATSON, Dorothy (Dolly)
Victoria pioneer,
died October 26, 1986
Q-086-06
48°30.388   123°22.733

Dorothy Watson was born in Victoria, a daughter of florist Arthur Woodward and his wife Adelaide, well known for the home they called "Clovelly."

Her husband Curtis Watson, a graduate of the Wright Brothers flying school in Dayton, Ohio, served in the First World War with the Royal Naval Air Service.

They were married in Victoria in 1917.

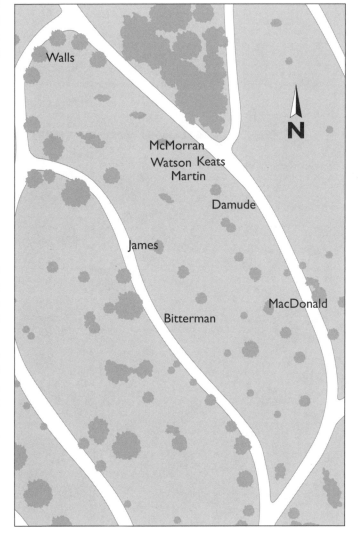

Section R

• Opened in 1983, this section was formerly part of the provincial government's game farm.

ADASKIN, Murray
Musician and composer, died May 6, 2002
R-035-36   48°30.535   123°22.811

Murray Adaskin was a Toronto-born violinist, composer, conductor and teacher.

He played violin in Toronto in silent film presentations, and was a violinist with the Toronto Symphony Orchestra from 1923 to 1936. From 1938 to 1952 he was with the Royal York Hotel trio.

He was head of the Department of Music at the University of Saskatchewan from 1952 to 1966, including four years as conductor of the Saskatoon Symphony Orchestra.

He then became the Composer-in-Residence until 1972, the first position of its type at a Canadian university. After that he retired to Victoria.

He died just before the release of the first two CDs of a five-disc collection of his work.

ERICKSON, Kjell Edward
Accident victim,
died August 10, 1992
R-036-06
48°30.539   123°22.805

Kjell Edward Erickson was just 14 years old when he died in a motor vehicle accident near Morinville, Alberta.

His tombstone has 51 words – including adventurer, comedian, energetic, independent and unlucky – to sum up a life that ended too soon.

HALL, Leon Edward
Sports scorekeeper, died January 11, 1985
R-062-20   48°30.556   123°22.800

Leon Edward Hall was a familiar figure at Victoria's Memorial Arena from its opening in 1949 until his death at the age of 64. He was considered to be the top scorekeeper and statistician in the area, working both hockey and lacrosse games.

Hall declined an offer to become league statistician for the old professional Western Hockey League because it would have required him to leave Victoria. He also turned down an opening in the National Hockey League that would have seen him move to Montreal.

When not at the arena, Hall worked for Canada Post before becoming director of postal services for the provincial government.

HILBORN, William Harold
Seafood businessman, died October 30, 1984
R-078-32   48°30.581   123°22.801

William Harold Hilborn founded Oakland Industries in 1960. He was one of the first to recognize the potential of the herring-roe industry for the Japanese market. The company collapsed under its debt load in 1977.

After that, Hilborn built a new business, Pacific Seafoods in Sidney, concentrating on smoked salmon. His life spiralled down, however, and ended in a shootout with police at his home.

STOREY, William Howard (Bill)
Air Canada pilot, died August 24, 1985
R-065-39   48°30.562   123°22.815

William Howard (Bill) Storey lived in Manitoba until three years before he died, but his job took him much farther afield. For 35 years, he was a pilot with Air Canada. The marker on his grave features an airplane, reflecting his career.

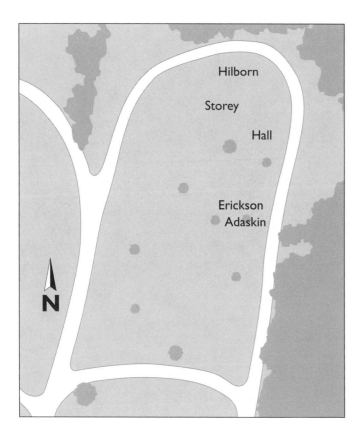

Section S

GALITZINE, Prince Nikita
Russian noble, died August 24, 2003
S-057-08   48°30.413   123°22.703

GALITZINE, Princess Blanche Eva Marion
Russian noble, died August 19, 1993
S-057-08   48°30.413   123°22.703

Prince Nikita Galitzine was a member of the Russian royal family. He was born in Dolzhik, southeast of Moscow, in 1912, the son of Prince Sergei Dimitrievich Galitzine and of his first wife, née Countess Zoë O'Rourke. Nikita married Blanche Eve Marion Pryor in London in 1949.

GUTOSKI, Anthony (Tony)
Curler, died November 13, 1996
S-048-20   48°30.396   123°22.665

Anthony (Tony) Gutoski represented B.C. at the 1958 Brier, the national men's curling championship. The Brier that year was in Victoria's Memorial Arena.

Gutoski had defeated Glen Harper of Duncan in the all-Island final to win the B.C. title and the right to compete in the Brier. Gutoski's rink of third Bill Dunstan, second Gary Leibel and lead Dale Dalziel finished 6-4 at the Brier that year to tie for fourth place. Matt Baldwin of Edmonton was the victor.

Gutoski, a native of Eden, Manitoba, won several big bonspiels. His success gave curling more exposure in Victoria in an era when the sport was dominated by prairie rinks. Gutoski was later well-known as the icemaker at the Victoria Curling Club.

HALL-CARRUTHERS, Dianne
Oilpatch pioneer, died October 13, 1995
S-035-23   48°30.398   123°22.689

The marker for Dianne Hall-Carruthers features an oil rig – a reminder of the way in which she blazed a trail to the top for female executives in the Calgary oilpatch.

Hall joined Nova Corp. in 1972 as executive assistant to president Bob Blair, and rose swiftly through the ranks to become a senior vice-president of the pipeline and utilities giant by 1978. At Nova, Hall – known as Dianne Narvik, her first married name, at the time – was in the thick of the "big pipeline battles" in the 1970s.

Foothills Pipelines Ltd., backed by Nova and Westcoast Energy Inc., won the battle to build the pipeline from Caroline, Alberta, to the United States Midwest. Nova's acquisition of Husky Oil Ltd. followed just a few years later. Hall also served as a director on the boards of Coca-Cola Canada and the Montreal-based Laurentian Group Corp.

Hall left Nova in 1987 and moved to the coast where she owned and operated Sea Island Air Ltd. with her husband, Bob Carruthers.

McKINNON, Allan Bruce
Federal politician, died September 19, 1990
S-079-24   48°30.441   123°22.690

Allan Bruce McKinnon served as defence minister in Joe Clark's Progressive Conservative government of 1979 and 1980. He was the MP for Victoria from 1972 to 1988.

McKinnon was the Tory defence critic for 10 years. He said on retirement that his greatest regret had been Robert Stanfield's failure to win the 1974 general election.

Born in Saskatchewan, McKinnon spent much of the Depression riding the rails.

WRIGHT, Walter Percival (Percy)
Provincial politician, died September 1, 1992
S-024-33   48°30.371   123°22.667

Walter Percival (Percy) Wright had a role in one of the key events in the early years of W.A.C. Bennett's Social Credit government. Wright was elected as a Social Credit candidate in the provincial election in June 1953.

He resigned his safe Victoria seat in October so Einar Gunderson, Bennett's choice as finance minister, could win a spot in the legislature. It turned out that the seat wasn't all that safe. Gunderson lost, dashing Bennett's plan for a dream team in his cabinet. Gunderson's loss also caused Bennett to lose faith in the transferable ballot system of voting.

• At the top of the hill on the northeast side of the burial park. Opened in 1990.

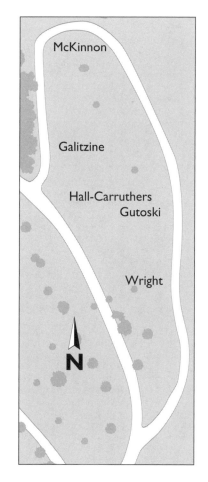

Section U

• Opened in 1996 on the game farm land acquired from the City of Victoria.

BROWN, Graham Stuart Lamont
Police chief, died June 29, 1998
U-042-31   48°30.490   123°22.892

Graham Stuart Lamont Brown attended Esquimalt secondary school, graduating in 1968. He played for the Victoria Cougars hockey team in 1968-69. Brown joined the Esquimalt police and fire department in 1971, and rose through the ranks to become chief in 1996. He died of cancer.

ENG, Henry
Grocery retailer, died June 10, 1997
U-018-08   48°30.467   123°22.915
ENG, Eddie Henry
"Woo Fat," died November 25, 2006
U-017-28   48°30.467   123°22.913

Henry Eng was born in Saanich and attended Cloverdale School. The family ran a market garden, and Eng spent his early years working there. In 1952 he set up a vegetable stand to sell the family's surplus produce. The stand evolved into Oakcrest Food Stores, the first major independent supermarket group in Victoria.

Nearby is the marker for Henry's son Eddie, a member of the Bounty Hunters motorcycle club known by his nickname, Woo Fat. After his father died, Eddie took over the business. He also restored vintage cars.

HILMY, Amin
Egyptian diplomat, died January 1, 2007
U-016-24   48°30.468   123°22.909

Amin Hilmy II was born in Cairo, Egypt, in 1916. During the Second World War he was the Egyptian liaison officer with British and Allied forces in Egypt co-ordinating the country's air defences against the German and Italian air campaign.

In 1954 he was put in charge of the implementation of the Anglo-Egyptian Evacuation Treaty from the Suez Canal region.

In 1960 he joined Egypt's foreign service, and in 1964 was appointed ambassador to the United Nations. In 1968 he was nominated ambassador to Canada, but was sent to New Delhi instead. He also became ambassador to Nepal and Vietnam. After a last stint as ambassador with the UN in New York, he retired in 1979 and moved to Canada, first to Ottawa and in 1988 to Victoria.

JORDAN, Gilbert Paul
"The boozing barber," died July 7, 2006
U-060-17   48°30.498   123°22.888

Gilbert Paul Jordan, who ran a barbershop in Abbotsford for many years, was notorious for plying women with deadly doses of alcohol. He became known as "the boozing barber" for his actions.

Jordan was convicted of manslaughter in 1988 for providing a woman with so much alcohol that she died with a blood-alcohol level of .91, more than 11 times the legal limit of .08. Over the years, Jordan was in the company of at least seven women whose deaths were related to alcohol. Most of them were First Nations women, and poor.

LARGE, Robert John
Grocery retailer, died December 28, 1999
U-14-26   48°30.465   123°22.900
LARGE, Claudette Mae
Murder victim, died April 26, 1980
U-14-25   48°30.465   123°22.900

Claudette Mae Large was murdered in Hawaii in 1980. Her husband Robert was charged in connection with her death, but was acquitted on the grounds of insanity.

Robert was a partner with his brothers in two grocery companies that filed for bankruptcy in 1984. Before they failed, the companies had stores in Duncan, Parksville, Ganges and Port Hardy. Claudette was originally buried in another part of the burial park, but after Robert died, she was moved so they could be together again.

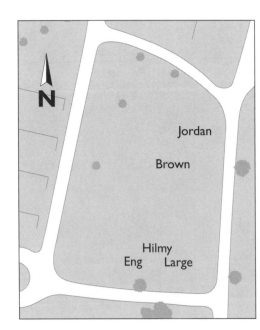

Section W

ASKEW, Prosper
Catholic priest, died August 17, 2004
W-027-26   48°30.549   123°22.887

Monsignor Prosper Askew was born in France in 1925, and felt the call to the priesthood when he was in his teens. Ordained in 1953, he was appointed chaplain to the pope in 1972.

He lived in a variety of places in Europe and the Middle East. He spoke half a dozen modern languages including Arabic. He worked as a programmer of daily news bulletins at Vatican radio in Rome and published several theological studies.

When Askew moved to Victoria in the early 1980s, he became a member of the faculty and professor of French at what was then Royal Roads Military College, where he taught for several years before retiring.

He also served as the president of the St. Camillus Association of B.C., a society that intervenes on behalf of seniors who are being abused in institutions or by their families.

SMITH, Melvin
Government adviser, died September 3, 2000
W-024-18   48°30.557   123°22.881

Melvin Smith was a leading constitutional expert and B.C. advocate. He served as constitutional advisor to four successive B.C. premiers, then left government service in 1991 to become a commentator on public affairs and a university lecturer.

Smith wrote the 1995 book, Our Home or Native Land?, which attacked the provincial government's treaty process. Smith argued provincial governments were giving away too much land to aboriginals. He opposed any granting of rights — such as fishing or logging rights — to aboriginals based on their ethnicity.

In 1992, Smith became one of the most outspoken opponents of the Charlottetown Accord, urging British Columbians to vote "no" in a national referendum on the constitutional deal.

His printed opposition to the Charlottetown Accord was reprinted and distributed in the tens of thousands across Western Canada, offering analytical support for the No forces.

WINTER, Jack
Hollywood screenwriter, died December 29, 2006
W-042-05   48°30.561   123°22.921

Jack Winter graduated from Harvard in 1962 after majoring in philosophy and writing for the Harvard Lampoon. He became a comedy writer. In 1965 he became the youngest writer to win the Television-Radio Writer's Annual Award.

Winter wrote for many early television sitcoms, including The Dick Van Dyke Show, The Mary Tyler Moore Show, Laverne and Shirley, The Odd Couple, Happy Days and The Monkees. He was also credited with a few movies, including Big and Awakenings.

Winter was slightly eccentric. It was said that he supported himself for a year by placing bets on basketball games. He ran a business importing and selling Turkish rugs. He collected frogs. He retired in 2001 and moved to Victoria to work on his book, The Answer to Everything.

Winter's grave, in keeping with Muslim tradition, does not have a marker.

• Opened in 2000. This was the first section since D Extension to allow upright memorials. It also has a distinctive feature wall.

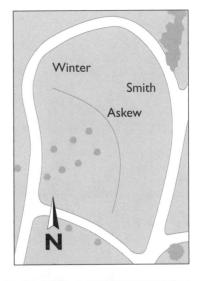

Mausoleum

• The Mausoleum, offering interment in raised niches, was opened in 1996.

SZONGOTT, Gottfried
Scientist, died April 28, 1999

Gottfried Szongott developed the mechanical components of a revolutionary film transport system to be used in nuclear event photography or in large data storage machines.

While at Stanford University in California, he also worked on a film digitizing system that would allow for automatic analysis of films produced in high-energy nuclear experiments.

VON KORNFELDT, Kurt Paul
Naval officer, died July 24, 1999

Kurt Paul Von Kornfeldt enlisted in the United States Navy in 1990, and was the recipient of several awards and medals.

He was on his way to Point Mugu Naval Air Station to report for reserve duty when he was killed on Highway 101 in Thousand Oaks, California.

His car was struck by another vehicle. Both drivers got out of their cars after the collision, and both were struck and killed by other vehicles.

Von Kornfeldt was entombed with full United States military honours, including a 21-gun salute. A large honour guard and contingents of navy personnel were bussed to the cemetery for the service.

Garden of Remembrance

BAKER, Shirley
CUSO director, died June 3, 1995
Garden C-362   48°30.149   123°22.969

Shirley Baker, born in Saskatoon, was the co-ordinator of women's activities at the University of Victoria, and later was appointed manager of housing services.

She had earlier worked on research in the Banting Institute in Toronto and the Borden Company in Toronto and New York. She lived for 18 years in Africa, where her husband John was a geologist, until his death there in 1963.

In Victoria she worked at UVic from 1965-83. She was involved in the professional women's Zonta Club, Canadian University Service Overseas, YM-YWCA and Pearson College.

In 1968 she went to Tanzania as CUSO regional director for east and central Africa. In 1973, CUSO in Tanzania created the Shirley Baker Project to fund a CUSO clinic.

CAMERON, James Oscar
Victoria businessman, died October 20, 1943
Garden B-247   48°30.141   123°22.963

James Oscar Cameron came to Victoria in 1907 and formed the Cameron Lumber Company. He also ran a securities company.

Born in Tennessee, Cameron was called to the bar in his home state, Texas and New Mexico. After moving to British Columbia, he became involved in the Victoria Board of Trade and the Victoria Chamber of Commerce.

GRAVLIN, Doris Charnock Thomson
Murder victim and ghost, September 22, 1936
Garden C-100   48°30.152   123°22.962

Doris Charnock Thomson Gravlin was born in England, and came to Canada as a 10-year-old with her mother after her father died. She worked as a nurse in Victoria.

Gravlin was beaten and strangled by her estranged husband, Victor Richard Gravlin, with her body hidden on the Victoria Golf Club links. Her husband then committed suicide by drowning.

There have been several reports that she is still with us. She has been seen on the golf course as well as on Beach Drive, adjacent to the course. She is usually wearing a white dress or brown business attire.

HEMBROFF-SCHLEICHER, Edythe May
Author and artist, died April 19, 1994
Garden C-186   48°30.151   123°22.965

Edythe May Hembroff-Schleicher was an artist, and a friend and biographer of painter Emily Carr. As a child she came to Victoria and attended Victoria High School.

• An area for cremated remains. The Garden of Remembrance, on the south side of the crematorium, was opened in 1939, and included four sections. The Garden was expanded in 1953 with sections E through P, and again in 1991 with sections Q through V.

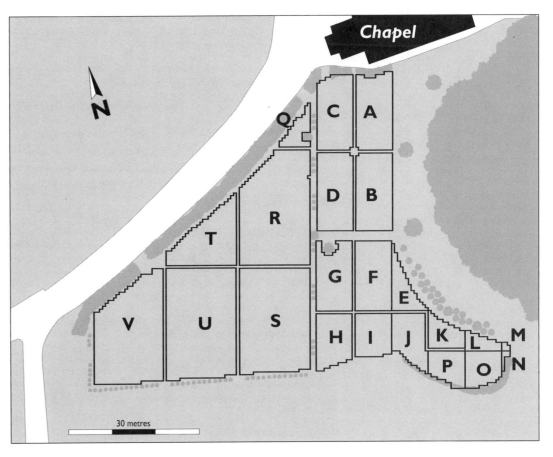

She studied art in San Francisco and Paris before returning to B.C., where she met Carr and sketched with her in the 1930s. She also met her first husband Frederick Brand and the couple was instrumental in promoting Carr's work.

She later remarried, after meeting Dr. Schleicher in Ottawa, where the two worked during the war years at the Department of Prisoner of War Censorship.

She wrote biographies about Carr after retiring to Victoria in the 1960s. Two of her paintings are in the Art Gallery of Greater Victoria collection. Under the signature of Edythe Hembroff Brand, her Portrait of Emily is in the Vancouver Art Gallery's permanent collection.

LaPOINTE, Richard Paul (Rick)
Hockey player, died October 17, 1999
Garden V-586   48°30.136   123°23.005

Richard Paul (Rick) LaPointe, who graduated from the Victoria Cougars to spend 12 seasons in the NHL, died of a heart attack at age 44. He was a lanky defenceman who used his powerful body to great advantage and carved a career with the Detroit Red Wings, Philadelphia Flyers, St. Louis Blues and Quebec Nordiques.

He scored 83 points for the Cougars and played a leading role for Canada at the 1975 world junior championships in Winnipeg. He was picked fifth overall by the Red Wings in the entry draft. LaPointe accumulated 229 points in his 710 NHL regular-season and playoff games.

McKENZIE, William Alexander
Provincial politician, died July 8, 1966
Garden K-170   48°30.124   123°22.955

William Alexander McKenzie played semi-professional baseball in Ontario in the 1890s, and moved to Penticton in 1903. There, he ran a fruit farm in the evenings and built houses by day. He moved to Victoria in 1928.

He was MLA from Similkameen from 1918 to 1934, and served as mines minister. He was 60 when he left politics, but started working as a carpenter in local shipyards.

In his 70s, McKenzie was superintendent of building construction on the Hope-Princeton Highway project. He finally retired at 85.

MILLIGAN, Wallace
Soccer coach, died December 9, 1997
Garden U-011   48°30.136   123°22.985

Wallace Milligan had a pro football (soccer) career in Scotland, playing for teams such as Airdrie, Dumbarton, Aldershot and East Stirling.

Then he noticed an ad in a Scottish newspaper asking for soccer players to play in British Columbia. In 1948 he arrived in New Westminster and two years later came across the strait to star for Victoria United of the old Pacific Coast Soccer League.

He was the playing coach for United when it beat English League champion Fulham in 1951 at Royal Athletic Park. Milligan became the coach of the successful United in the 1960s, and from 1966 to 1971 the first coach of the fledgling University of Victoria Vikes soccer program.

MORRIS, John William
Automobile dealer, died February 22, 1952
Garden C-233   48°30.152   123°22.963

John William Morris founded National Motors, making him a pioneer in the automobile industry in Victoria. He moved to the city in 1906.

MOUAT, Alexander Naismith
Provincial comptroller, died January 6, 1950
Garden D-143   48°30.147   123°22.967

Alexander Naismith Mouat, a veteran of the second Riel Rebellion, served for 20 years with the Hudson's Bay Company, and by 1899 was the company's chief inspector.

He served as comptroller in Edmonton, setting up an acclaimed audit system, before coming to British Columbia in 1916 to become the province's first comptroller-general

OLDFIELD, Henry Clarence
Saanich pioneer, died March 31, 1966
Garden E-262   48°30.132   123°22.960

Henry Clarence Oldfield was one of the first school commissioners, responsible for ensuring that children were attending classes. He later became a school trustee.

He was also a key factor in the creation of the Fruit

Growers' Association, which worked to obtain higher prices for farmers. The organization bought a cannery in the Lake Hill district, a move that led to the establishment on Quadra Street of the B.C. Growers' Winery, the first in British Columbia.

Oldfield was one of the key proponents of the Royal Oak Burial Park, and helped to convince investors to buy the debentures used to pay for the project.

PATTULLO, Thomas Dufferin (Duff)
British Columbia premier, died March 29, 1956
Garden C-006   48°30.154   123°22.961

Thomas Dufferin (Duff) Pattullo was British Columbia's premier from 1933 to 1941. He was the Liberal MLA for Prince Rupert for 29 years, from 1916 through 1945.

Duff Pattullo was born in Ontario, and worked as a newspaperman before the lure of Klondike gold pulled him to the Yukon.

He moved to Prince Rupert after the gold rush ended.

As premier, he hatched a plan for B.C. to annex the Yukon, prompting old-timers in Dawson to threaten his life if he dared to go there. In response, Pattullo hired an airplane, flew to the Yukon, and stared down his opponents, earning their respect in the process.

After his election defeat in 1945, Pattullo chose to remain in Victoria.

Pattullo Bridge in New Westminster is named after him.

SALMON, Henry Louis
Tobacconist and firefighter, died April 22, 1958
Garden E-293   48°30.129   123°22.959

Henry Louis Salmon came to Victoria in 1884, started a tobacco store, and volunteered for the fire department. The following year the fire department starting paying its firefighters, and Salmon divided his time between the store and the department.

Over the years, he expanded his store several times before selling it to C.A. Steele. He then retired to a house he built on the Saanich Inlet, and became known for the lemons he grew.

SHERET, Andrew
Plumbing businessman, died September 12, 1947
Garden C-223   48°30.149   123°22.967

Andrew Sheret started the business that bears his name in 1892. It was a wholesale distributor of plumbing and heating supplies. It had two stores when he died, and has been expanded considerably since then.

In 1943, he was honoured with a life membership in the American Society of Heating and Ventilating Engineers.

He was a member of the Victoria Board of Trade and the Victoria Chamber of Commerce for many years.

• The Garden of Remembrance in the early 1940s.

71

Grove of Remembrance

• An area for cremated remains, opened in 1965.

• Guides such as these are in every section, and can be used to find markers.

BUTTERFIELD, Frederick
Land surveyor, died February 14, 1948
Grove C-220   48°30.335   123°22.895

Frederick Butterfield came to Victoria in 1907 and practised as a land surveyor from 1912 until his death. One of his projects was Royal Oak Burial Park.

Butterfield was president of the Corporation of B.C. Land Surveyors when he died, and had served as its secretary from 1939 to 1946.

He was born in Ulverston, Lancashire.

FORBES, Elizabeth
Newspaper journalist, died February 8, 1981
Grove F-743   48°30.358   123°22.895

Elizabeth Forbes was born in Victoria in 1896, and started working at the Victoria Daily Times as a stenographer in the late 1920s.

She later sold advertising before becoming social editor when Nancy Hodges entered politics.

Forbes was social editor for 20 years, until she retired in 1964. She wrote regular columns until she died.

She was the author of Wild Roses At Their Feet, the story of Vancouver Island's pioneer women.

HILL, Esther Marjorie
Pioneer architect, died January 7, 1985
Grove N-935   48°30.339   123°22.856

Esther Marjorie Hill graduated from the University of Toronto in 1920 with a degree in architecture, the first woman to attain that degree.

She worked in Toronto and New York before moving to Alberta in 1925.

She moved to Victoria in 1936, but had to give up architecture because of ill health.

In the early 1950s she returned to the field and designed several homes, an apartment block, a motel and a garage before retiring again in 1963.

HODGES, Nancy (Sarah Annie)
Journalist and politician, died December 15, 1969
Grove A-973   48°30.355   123°22.908

Nancy (Sarah Annie) Hodges was the first female Speaker of the legislature in British Columbia — and in the British Commonwealth as well.

In her earlier career, as a journalist, Hodges had argued that more women should enter politics and serve in responsible positions.

Hodges worked as social editor of the Victoria Daily Times from 1916 to 1943. She was elected to the legislature in

1941, and was named Speaker in 1950. She lost her seat in 1952. She continued to write a column until 1953, despite her increasing activity in the political arena.

In 1953, Hodges was named to the Senate, and became a member of the divorce committee. She resigned from the Senate in 1965.

LUNEY, Walter
Commercial builder, died May 28, 1968
Grove B-018   48°30.353   123°22.914

Walter Luney narrowly escaped disaster in 1896 when he got off a crowded streetcar just before it crashed through Point Ellice Bridge into the water, killing 55 people. Later, he held the first driver's licence issued in British Columbia.

Luney ran a construction company responsible for many large projects, including more than half the schools built while he was in business, the main branches of the three banks, the Crystal Garden and the chapel and crematorium at Royal Oak Burial Park.

Luney's company built bridges, paved roads, and brought the Canadian National Railway line into Victoria. He and his brother owned the Point Hope Shipyards.

TICKLE, William Fletcher (Billy)
Empress Hotel musician, died August 7, 1974
Grove F-045   48°30.363   123°22.905

William Fletcher (Billy) Tickle led the Empress Hotel Trio for 32 years, charming customers at the afternoon tea. In the evenings, the Billy Tickle Empress Hotel Dance Band performed.

Tickle also played at Government House and with the Victoria Symphony Orchestra.

A veteran of the First World War, Tickle worked in the grocery business for many years.

WIGHTMAN, Cyril Merritt (Squi)
Military veteran, died April 7, 1991
Grove O-677   48°30.350   123°22.867

Cyril Merritt (Squi) Wightman sold advertising for the Daily Colonist and rose through the ranks to become assistant publisher. He then became a manager for Pacific Great East-

ern Railway, then the Public Service Commission of the provincial government.

He joined the Canadian Scottish Regiment in 1926 and was second in command of the battalion on D-Day in 1944. He was severely wounded a few days later.

In 1986 he was appointed an honorary colonel of the regiment.

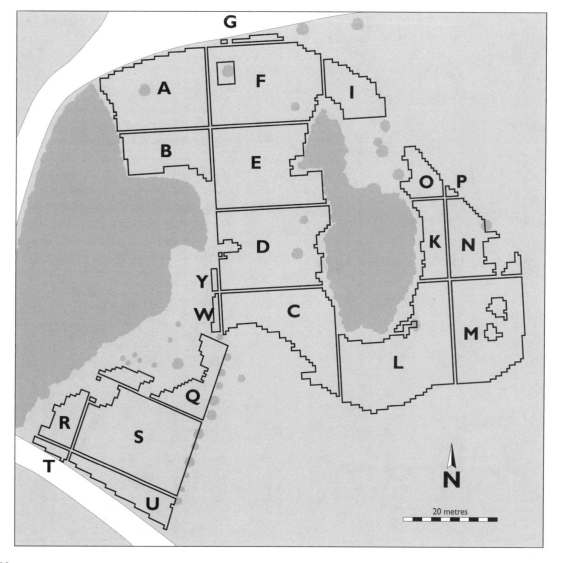

Island of Remembrance

DRISCOLL, Mabel Helen Fortune
Titanic survivor, died February 19, 1968
Island-C-613   48°30.369   123°22.817

Mabel Helen Fortune, a native of Winnipeg, was 23 when she boarded the Titanic for a voyage to North America. She was on her way home after a vacation in Europe because her family hoped that she would forget about a romance with Minnesota jazz artist Harrison Driscoll.

Her father and brother died when the Titanic sank. Mabel married Driscoll despite her family's wishes. They had a son and later divorced. Driscoll lived in Victoria for 47 years.

MARTIN, Elizabeth
Pioneer nurse, died February 12, 1965
Island-A-061   48°30.350   123°22.812

Elizabeth Martin was born in Edinburgh, but moved to Victoria in 1898. She graduated from the Royal Jubilee School of Nursing in 1906, and served overseas in the First World War with the No. 5 Canadian General Hospital.

STURDY, John Henry
Provincial politician, died September 20, 1966
Island-E-215   48°30.366   123°22.830

John Henry Sturdy was a cabinet minister in Tommy Douglas's first Co-operative Commonwealth Federation government in Saskatchewan, serving as minister of social welfare and assistant to the premier.

He retired to Victoria in 1960.

WORSLEY, Evelyn
Leper colony matron, died January 4, 1974
Island-C-624   48°30.370   123°22.815

Evelyn Worsley served as the matron at the Bentinck Island leper colony, just off Rocky Point, for the last five years before it closed in 1956. She said that she took the job because "nobody else would take it."

Worsley furnished the cottages in bright colours and insisted that the patients look after themselves and their gardens.

She was the widow of Col. George Stanley Worsley, who was buried in Section C.

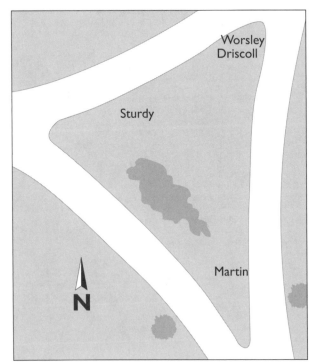

Columbarium Grove

ALDOUS, Montague (Monty)
B.C. Ferries manager, died June 19, 2002
Redwood D-5   48°30.382   123°22.891

Montague (Monty) Aldous started his working life in cookhouses in logging camps in the Campbell River area. He became manager of the B.C. Packers subsidiary, Packers Steamship, in 1955.

Aldous played a key role in the beginning of the B.C. Ferries service. He was appointed general manager in 1959, just before the service started. When he took the position, there were only two ferries in the fleet and the highways to the terminals at Swartz Bay and Tsawwassen had only two lanes.

He guided the business operations of the system until 1973, when he became a labour consultant. He retired in 1975.

ASH, Arthur James Richard
Columbarium advocate, died January 15, 1988
Rosewood A-11 48°30.386   123°22.893

Arthur James Richard Ash, who owned a shoe store on Government Street, served as a Liberal MLA from 1948 to 1952 before losing his seat to the Social Credit candidate. He then turned to municipal politics, and served as the Saanich reeve from 1956 to 1958.

Before moving to Saanich in 1946, Ash had served for nine years on the city council in Ottawa. He resigned as reeve to move to Nevada, where he worked as a representative of electrical contractors and served as a member of the National Council of Industrial Relations. He and his wife Marie returned to Greater Victoria in 1973.

Ash joined the cemetery board and lobbied for a columbarium grove. He got his wish, although he did not live to see it. Ash's ashes were the first placed in the grove when it opened on June 23, 1988.

BLACK, Wesley Drewett
Provincial politician, died January 10, 2000
Oakwood-B-46 48°30.380   123°22.893

Wesley Drewett Black was elected to the provincial legislature in 1952, the year that W.A.C. Bennett became premier. Black, who represented the Creston area, was quickly named to cabinet — and stayed there for the next 20 years.

He was one of Bennett's closest confidantes. He first sat at the cabinet table as provincial secretary. In subsequent years he became minister of municipal affairs, of social welfare, of health and hospital insurance, and finally minister of highways.

• Opened in 1988, this section provides spaces for cremated remains.

Memorial Woods

• Opened in 2002, the Memorial Woods has room for upright markers nestled among trees.

HUGHES, Monica Mary
Children's author, died March 7, 2003
Memorial Woods   48°30.384   123°22.881

Monica Mary Hughes was a prominent Edmonton-based author of many books for children.

Her works included Hunter in the Dark, a book about a boy with leukemia that won the Canada Council's Children's Literature Prize, and The Keeper of the Isis Light, a novel set in an alien world that spawned a best-selling trilogy which, in turn, won the prestigious Phoenix Award.

Hughes was considered to be the first science fiction writer for children in Canada.

Born in Liverpool in 1925, Hughes immigrated to Canada in 1952 and started writing in 1971. She published more than thirty-five novels in ten languages around the world.

She was also a two-time Governor General's Award winner, and in 2002 received the Order of Canada and the Queen's Golden Jubilee medal.

JOHNSTON, Douglas Millar
University professor, died May 6, 2006
Memorial Woods   48°30.392   123°22.891

Douglas Millar Johnston taught at the New School for Social Research in New York City, the University of Western Ontario, Louisiana State University, the University of Toronto, Dalhousie University, the National University of Singapore, and the University of Victoria in a career that lasted until 1999.

In retirement he held the titles of emeritus professor at UVic Law School and adjunct professor at Dalhousie Law School.

He wrote more than 30 books and 90 articles on the theory and history of international law, law of the sea, marine and environmental policy studies, comparative law, modern Chinese studies and public policy issues.

Johnston created the Southeast Asian Programme in Ocean Law, Policy and Management (SEAPOL) centred in Bangkok, the Dalhousie Ocean Studies Programme (DOSP) in Halifax and the Maritime Awards Society of Canada (MASC) dedicated to student scholarships. He was the founding Chair in Asia-Pacific Relations at the University of Victoria.

Cremated – no marker

ABKHAZI, Prince Nicholas
Garden founder, died December 25, 1987
ABKHAZI, Princess Peggy
Garden founder, died November 14, 1994

Princess Peggy Abkhazi, a former prisoner of war, lived in Victoria for nearly half a century.

Widow of Prince Nicholas Abkhazi of Georgia, the princess was born Marjorie Mabel Carter in Shanghai in 1902 and was educated in England and Paris.

During the Second World War, she spent 3 1/2 years in a Japanese prison camp in Shanghai. Following her release, she came to Victoria to recuperate. She purchased an acre of wild land on Fairfield Road and married a Georgian prince she had met in Paris. Together they began growing a garden that became internationally known.

The garden contained rhododendrons, azaleas, hybrid brooms, choice conifers, Japanese maples and ornamental lily ponds surrounded by outcroppings of rocks and old Garry oak trees.

ANDERSEN, Helen
Artist and activist, died December 23, 1995

Helen Andersen was born in Winnipeg, the daughter of a physician, and grew up in a house filled with Indian art. She worked as a nurse and moved to Vancouver where she began her art training.

Andersen moved to Victoria in 1980. She was a student of the Victoria College of Art and played an active role in the Saanich Peninsula Arts and Crafts Society. The evolution of Andersen's paintings culminated in a series of bright and expressive canvases about natives and women.

She was also a peace activist, and received a special prize for her efforts at a conference in Warsaw in 1987.

ARMSTRONG, Charles Nesbitt Frederick
Madam Melba's husband, died November 2, 1948

Charles Nesbitt Frederick Armstrong was born the sixth son of an Irish baronet, Armstrong of Gallen, in Kings Coun-

ty, Ireland. He lived for many years at Shawnigan Lake after a career that included horse ranching in Australia, commercial fishing in New Orleans, and sailing.

His real claim to fame was his marriage. His wife from 1882 to 1900 was Helen Porter Mitchell, better known as Madame Melba, the Australian singer. Two foods, Peach Melba and Melba Toast, were named after her, and for a few years a Melba doll was popular among children.

ARMSTRONG, David Montgomery
Radio pioneer, died April 22, 1985

David Armstrong founded AM radio station CKDA – the DA representing his initials – in 1950. In 1954 he won approval for British Columbia's first FM radio station, CKDA-FM. In 1956 he started CHEK Television – he was denied permission to call it CKDA-TV – but sold the station in 1960.

CKDA was moved to the FM band in 2000, and its name has changed a couple of times. CKDA-FM was known for a few years as CFMS-FM, and then CIOC-FM, the Ocean.

CHEK is still CHEK.

AUSTIN, John Gardiner
Military officer, died November 2, 1956

Brig.-Gen. John Gardiner Austin served as the inspector of army ordnance services in Britain before retiring to Victoria in 1929.

Born in Barbados, Austin was educated at the Royal Military Academy in Woolwich, England, and obtained a commission in the Royal Army in 1891.

Austin served as the president of the Red Cross Society, Victoria branch, during the Second World War.

BOYD, Edwin Alonzo
Bank robber, died May 16, 2002

Edwin Alonzo Boyd was one of the most notorious bank robbers in Canadian history. In 1952, when he was captured, he was considered to be Canada's Public Enemy Number One.

• The ashes of the Abkhazis were scattered on their gardens.

Boyd was a veteran of the Second World War who drove a streetcar, then decided that robbing banks might be an easier way to make a living. Working solo at first, then with partners, he pulled off a variety of heists in the Toronto area.

After his release from prison in 1966, he moved to Greater Victoria and settled into a quiet life with a new name.

• The ashes of the Butcharts were scattered in Tod Inlet.

BROWNING, Archie
Top athlete, died November 18, 1989

Archie Browning made his mark as a lacrosse player in the 1940s and 1950s. He was a member of three Mann Cup teams – the New Westminster Adanacs in 1947 and the Victoria Shamrocks in 1955 and 1957. He was also a curler.

Browning was a member of the Esquimalt police and fire department for 27 years, retiring in 1982 as a sergeant.

His name lives on with the Archie Browning sports centre in Esquimalt.

BUTCHART, Jennie Foster
Butchart Gardens, died December 12, 1950
BUTCHART, Robert Pim
Butchart Gardens, died October 27, 1943

Robert Pim and Jennie Foster Butchart were responsible for the world-famous gardens on the Saanich Peninsula.

Robert started the first Portland cement plant in Canada in 1886, and soon had a financial interest in factories across Canada and in the United States. He served on the boards of many companies in both countries.

Jennie started the Butchart Gardens in 1904 to hide the ugliness of the cement pit excavations close to her home. Landscaping over shapeless masses of limestone, she planted thousands of plants, obtained from all parts of the world, and transformed the pits into a floral showpiece.

By the time she died in 1950, the gardens were drawing an estimated 50,000 visitors a year.

CASEY, Joseph William
Saanich reeve, died August 20, 1974

Joseph William Casey served as the reeve of Saanich from 1949 to 1955. He was credited with getting the municipality a drainage and sewerage system.

While living in Victoria in the 1920s he ran for city council, but was not successful. He also sought office as a Social Credit candidate in the 1957 federal election, but did not win.

In 1968, he was appointed the first senator of Royal Jubilee Hospital, in recognition of his 15 years of service to the hospital board.

CHETWYND, William Ralph Talbot
Provincial politician, died April 3, 1957

William Ralph Talbot Chetwynd was a member of W.A.C. Bennett's Social Credit cabinet from 1952 until his death in 1957. He helped promote the expansion of the Pacific Great Eastern Railway north of Prince George, and in his honour the people of Little Prairie changed the name of their community to Chetwynd.

Chetwynd came to British Columbia from England in 1908, and started a ranch at Walhachin, in the Thompson River Valley west of Kamloops. After serving in the First World War, he returned to find Walhachin virtually abandoned. He then worked for the Douglas Lake Cattle Company near Merritt, owned a sheep ranch and worked for the PGE before being elected to the government.

CHIRINSKY-CHIKHMATOFF, Princess Jenny
A Butchart, a noble, died January 16, 1971

Jenny Chirinsky-Chikhmatoff was born a Butchart, a daughter of the man who created a cement works near Brentwood Bay and the woman who planted flowers there.

Jenny worked closely with her mother, Jennie, to create the Butchart Gardens, which became a world-famous tourist attraction.

Her first husband was Harry Ross, who died in his early 40s. Jenny Butchart Ross then married a member of the Russian nobility, which entitled her to use the term princess.

CHRISTIE, Albert Edward
Military veteran, died July 3, 1954

Major Albert Edward Christie served in the Riel Rebellion, the Boer War and the First World War. He was a former member of the 67th Battalion, Western Scots.

Christie was awarded the Distinguished Service Order.

CLEARIHUE, Joseph Badenoch
Politician, judge, died August 6, 1976

Joseph Badenoch Clearihue served as a soldier, politician and judge, and is also known as the leading force behind the creation of the University of Victoria. In 1963 he became UVic's first chancellor and first chairman of its board of governors.

The first building erected on the Gordon Head campus bears his name.

Clearihue was a member of the inaugural graduating class of Victoria College in 1903. He served in the First World War, winning the Military Cross for his efforts. He later served as an MLA and on Victoria city council. He practised law from 1916 to 1952, then served as a judge for 10 years.

CONACHER, Roy Gordon
Hockey player, died December 29, 1984

Roy Gordon Conacher played 11 seasons for the Boston Bruins, Chicago Blackhawks and Detroit Red Wings, mainly in the 1940s. He led the league in scoring in 1948-1949, with 26 goals and 42 assists.

He won the Art Ross Trophy that year, and in his career, he scored 226 goals.

He lived, however, in the shadows of two of his brothers — Lionel Conacher, Canada's outstanding athlete of the first half of the 20th century, and Charlie Conacher, a member of the famous Kid Line for the Toronto Maple Leafs.

Conacher lived in Victoria for the last two years of his life. He was posthumously inducted into the veteran category of the Hockey Hall of Fame in 1998.

COSMATOS, George Pan
Film director, died April 19, 2005

George Pan Cosmatos was a Greek who was born in Italy and grew up in Egypt and Cyprus. He spoke six languages.

After studying film in London, Cosmatos was assistant director to Otto Preminger on Exodus in 1960. He also worked on Zorba the Greek in 1964, The Cassandra Crossing in 1976, and Escape to Athena in 1979.

Cosmatos was nominated for a 1985 Golden Raspberry Award for directing Rambo: First Blood Part II. He won praise for Tombstone, a 1993 Western about Doc Holliday and Wyatt Earp.

COURTNALL, Archie Lawton
Hockey dad, died August 6, 1978

Archie Lawton Courtnall killed himself after struggling with depression for a year.

Courtnall's children, including former National Hockey League players Russ and Geoff, devoted themselves to raising money for psychiatric emergency care facilities at Royal Jubilee Hospital. The Archie Courtnall Centre, which opened in 2004, is their lasting tribute to their late father.

CUNNINGHAM, Jeffree Aikin
College educator, died April 22, 1974

Jeffree Aikin Cunningham was a native Victorian and student of Victoria College in 1906 and 1907. Cunningham became a biology instructor at Victoria College in 1924 and headed the biology department until his retirement in 1951.

From 1933 to 1944 he served as college registrar and from 1944 to 1951 was vice-principal. For his contributions to the institution, he received the University of Victoria's first honourary LLD degree in 1964. The Cunningham Building at UVic is named after him.

DEAN, John
Victoria pioneer, died March 28, 1943

One of the most famous headstones in Ross Bay Cemetery is that of John Dean, who had it put in place seven years before he died. He then posed for photographs beside the stone, showing off the inscription "It is a rotten world; artful politicians are its baine; it's saving grave is the artlessness of the young and the wonders of the sky."

Dean lived in Esquimalt, campaigned on city matters in Victoria, owned land on Mount Newton, died in Vancouver, was cremated in Saanich, and buried in Victoria. He is remembered best today by John Dean Park, the 80-acre oasis that he donated to the province. The park contains some of the last old-growth Douglas fir and Garry Oak stands on the Saanich Peninsula.

• The ashes of John Dean were interred in Ross Bay Cemetery.

DEELEY, Frederick Trevor (Trev)
Motorcycle dealer, died March 28, 2002
DEELEY, Joyce
Hospital benefactor, died March 25, 2001

Frederick Trevor (Trev) Deeley was chairman and founding member of Fred Deeley Imports, exclusive Harley Davidson distributors for Canada. He loved motorcycles and he raced, rode, repaired, collected, customized, sold, distributed and talked about motorcycles.

In 2001 he donated $1 million to the B.C. Cancer Foundation's Daring to Believe campaign to build a cancer research centre at the B.C. Cancer Agency's Vancouver Island Centre. This gift was made in honour of Joyce, who was then fighting cancer.

The Deeleys both named the B.C. Cancer Foundation as a beneficiary in their wills. After Trev died, it was announced that he had left more than five million dollars to the cancer foundation. The Trev and Joyce Deeley Research Centre was officially named in 2003.

EVE, Cecil Harold
Airline pioneer, died April 25, 1956
EVE, James Ernest
Airline pioneer, died August 24, 1957

The Eve brothers, Cecil Harold and James Ernest, opened an automobile dealership in Victoria in the 1920s selling Graham-Paige cars. They also founded B.C. Airways in 1928, providing the first flights linking Seattle and Vancouver to Victoria, using the old Lansdowne airfield. The service was suspended after a few weeks because of the crash of their Ford Tri-Motor airplane on the Washington coast.

Cecil Harold Eve was one of the first people in Victoria to use his own aircraft for hunting trips.

James Ernest Eve was an athlete, veteran of the British cavalry, breaker of wild Cariboo horses, test pilot, movie actor and provincial policeman.

GONNASON, Aaron
Lumber businessman, died December 27, 1938

Aaron Gonnason was born near Stockholm, Sweden in 1865, and came to Victoria in the 1880s. With his brother and a partner, he founded the lumber firm of Lemon, Gonnason and Company, and served as its president.

Gonnason was also a member of the Victoria Chess Club and the Uplands Golf Club.

GRAVES, Herbert Sandham
Newspaper editor, died October 10, 1972

Herbert Sandham Graves was editor of the Daily Colonist for 17 years. He first joined the newspaper staff in 1919, after returning from fighting in the First World War in France, Belgium and Palestine.

In 1921, Graves went to the Victoria Daily Times, and in 1929 was assigned the legislature beat. In 1931 he returned to the Colonist as legislature reporter, and remained in that position until 1942. During the Second World War, Graves wrote Lost Diary, an eyewitness account of the First World War. He was editor of the Colonist from 1943 to 1960.

HART, Edward Charles
Doctor and coroner, died October 31, 1960

Edward Charles Hart conducted more than 5,000 inquests and inquiries in more than half a century as Victoria's coroner. He graduated from McGill University in 1894, and practiced medicine in the Maritimes for two years before coming to Victoria.

He served in the army reserve before the First World War, and joined the regular army in 1914. He was awarded the Companion of St. Michael and St. George for his work overseas. He is also remembered as the owner of one of the first motor cars in Victoria – an Oldsmobile that he bought in 1903. He claimed he could get from his Cadboro Bay home to Esquimalt in just 17 minutes.

HILTON, Warren
Psychologist, author, died August 4, 1958

Warren Hilton travelled the world many times before choosing Victoria as his home. He lived here for the last 20 years of his life.

Born in St. Louis, Missouri, Hilton graduated from Harvard and Washington University. He studied law and was a financial advisor to large corporations.

• The ashes of Rev. Canon Harry Stocken (page 85) were interred on the Blackfoot reserve in Alberta.

He made his name in applied psychology, as the author of several books, including Driving Power of Thought. He was one of the few Victoria residents to have earned an entry in Who's Who In America.

HOLMES, Henry Cuthbert
Business leader, died May 23, 1968

Major Henry Cuthbert Holmes retired from the Pemberton, Holmes real estate office in 1965. He was a former president of the Victoria Real Estate Board, a Victoria alderman, a president of the Victoria and Island Tourist Bureau and a past-president of the Associated Chambers of Commerce of Vancouver Island. He was also on the advisory board of the Greater Victoria Art Gallery.

He was born in Madras, India, and served in the First World War.

HOLMES, Philip Despard Pemberton (Pip)
Honorary aide de camp, died May 18, 2007

Philip Despard Pemberton (Pip) Holmes descended from two famous Victoria families. He was the son of Major Henry Cuthbert Holmes and Philippa Despard Pemberton.

He joined the RCAF at the age of 17 and flew 33 missions in the Second World War.

He left the service with the rank of Squadron Leader, Flight Commander, and a proud holder of the Distinguished Flying Cross and other battle awards. After the war he joined the pioneer real estate and property management firm of Pemberton, Holmes Limited, founded by his great-grandfather, Joseph Despard Pemberton, in 1887.

In 1960 he was appointed honourary aide de camp to the Lieutenant Governor of British Columbia, Clarence Wallace, and held the position until 1963. In 1978 he was again appointed to the position, and served every lieutenant governor from Henry P. Bell-Irving to Iona Campagnolo.

IRELAND, Willard Ernest
Archivist and librarian, died January 27, 1979

Willard Ernest Ireland served as the provincial librarian and provincial archivist. He received honorary degrees from both the University of British Columbia and the University of Victoria. Ireland was born in Vancouver, and worked as a teacher before becoming the provincial archivist in 1940. He retired in 1974.

He was a member of the University of Victoria's board of governors, and was honorary secretary of the B.C. Centennial Committee from 1956 to 1959.

JOHNSON, Byron Ingemar (Boss)
British Columbia premier, died January 12, 1964

Byron Ingemar (Boss) Johnson was born and raised in Victoria, represented the city in the provincial legislature, and served as premier of British Columbia for five years, from 1947 to 1952.

Johnson's government introduced compulsory health insurance and a provincial sales tax, set at three per cent. It also worked on the development of the province, including the highway system, the Pacific Great Eastern Railway, and the Kenny Dam on the Nechako River. It was the largest earth-filled dam in the world, and was part of the first major hydroelectric project in B.C.

KERMODE, Francis
Anthropologist, died December 29, 1946

Francis Kermode was one of Canada's leading anthropologists. He served with the provincial government for 50 years, retiring as director of the Museum of Natural History in 1940.

Kermode's primary interest was in Coast Indian lore, and he supervised the erection of a native village at Belleville and Douglas streets. His name lives on in Ursus Kermodei, a white bear. His name was also given to a mountain in the Queen Charlotte Islands (Haida Gwaii).

KING, Freeman Foard
Wildlife expert, died September 26, 1975

Freeman Foard King – known as The Skipper to his many friends – was a self-taught naturalist who guided thousands of children in nature rambles.

He worked at Goldstream Provincial Park until he was 84 years old. Before that, he fought on behalf of Pacific Rim National Park and for the salmon that spawn in Goldstream.

• The ashes of Byron Johnson were buried at Ross Bay Cemetery.

Freeman King Park was named after him. It was later combined with Francis Park to become known as the Francis/King Park, and is administered by the Capital Regional District.

King was also involved in Scouting. He helped form the First West Sussex Scout troop in 1908, when he was 17. Thirty-four years after his work in England, King became the professional leader of the Victoria district's Scouts and Cubs.

• The ashes of Richard Layritz were placed under a tree on his property.

LAYRITZ, Richard Emil
Master gardener, died September 10, 1954

Richard Emil Layritz went to horticultural school in Stuttgart, worked for a time with the Dresden parks department, and gained further experience at the Ludwig Späth nursery in Berlin, the largest in Europe at the time.

Layritz arrived in Victoria in 1889 and made a down payment on 10 acres of virgin bush.

He went to the Klondike for the gold rush in 1898, and returned with a bankroll large enough to pay his debts and get his business rolling.

Within a short time he was growing thousands of different kinds of plants, shrubs and trees on his 70-acre estate and was shipping them all over North America and Europe. Layritz became a horticulturalist of world stature.

MACNICOL, Robert
Saanich reeve, died July 18, 1961

Robert Macnicol was the Saanich reeve from 1924 through 1926. A First World War veteran who was wounded at the Somme, Macnicol also served as overseas manager of Canadian Legion war services in Britain in 1941 and 1942 and was assistant general manager in Ottawa in 1943 and 1944.

He also was a justice of the peace, a member of the veterans' assistance commission, and president of the B.C. Command of the legion.

MARTIN, Archer Evan
Chief justice, died September 1, 1941

Archer Martin, born in Ontario, was called to the bar in Manitoba in 1887, and to the bar in British Columbia in 1894. He was appointed to the Supreme Court in 1897, at 33, and was elevated to the appeal court when it was created in 1909.

In 1937 Martin was named Chief Justice, and held the position until 1940. He was required to retire because he had reached 75 years of age.

McMULLIN, John Hugh
Police commissioner, died May 11, 1943

Col. John Hugh McMullin was commissioner of the British Columbia Provincial Police for 20 years. He introduced the divisional system of territorial supervision as well as new technology such as radios and motor patrols.

Born in Madras, India, he served in the Boer War. During the First World War he was in charge of recruitment in northern British Columbia. A son, Francis Hugh, was killed in action in 1942.

McPHERSON, Thomas Shanks
Businessman and philanthropist, died December 3, 1962

Thomas Shanks McPherson piled up a small fortune through shrewd investments, and then gave it away – after he died.

Born in Scotland in 1872, McPherson came to Canada when he was 10. After working in California, he came to Victoria in 1905. He opened the Central Building with a partner in 1912, and increased his investments many times over the years.

At his death, he owned the old Pantages theatre, now known as McPherson Playhouse. His name is also on the main library building at the University of Victoria, which was one of the major beneficiaries of his will.

MILES, Walter Sebastian
Businessman, died April 6, 1956

Walter Sebastian Miles was known as an expert on transportation. He was 15 when he started as an office boy with the Great Northern Railway, which operated the Victoria-Sidney railway and a car barge service between Sidney and New Westminster. He was an agent for steamship and railway companies for many years.

Miles – a grandson of Walter Miles, one of the earliest settlers on Vancouver Island – had been the chief sidesman at

Christ Church Cathedral for many years. More than 1,500 people attended his funeral at the cathedral. It was said to be the largest funeral in Victoria to that date.

MOLSON, William Hobart
Aide de camp, died November 12, 1951

William Hobart Molson was the senior aide de camp at Government House when he died. He was a descendant of John Molson, who founded the Molson banking and brewing interests in Montreal.

Molson came to Victoria to retire in 1926, but went to work at Government House instead. Over the next 25 years he served seven lieutenant-governors.

Molson won the Military Cross at the Battle of Arras in 1918. He was a flying officer, serving in British Columbia, for the Royal Canadian Air Force in the Second World War.

NESBITT, James Knight
Journalist and historian, died September 27, 1981

James Knight Nesbitt was the dean of the press gallery at the British Columbia legislature, but he was possibly better known as a historian.

In 1937, while working for the Victoria Daily Times, Nesbitt was assigned to interview everyone in Victoria who had been in the city when it was incorporated 75 years earlier. That sparked Nesbitt's interest in the past, and he devoted much of the next 44 years to bringing history back to life.

Nesbitt was the founder of the Craigdarroch Castle Preservation and Restoration Society. He staged a sleep-in at the legislature to protect historic tiles that were threatened with removal. He also fought on behalf of the markers at Ross Bay Cemetery when a plan to "beautify" the cemetery was raised.

NICHOLSON, George Salier Willis
Prohibition rum-runner, died January 9, 1980

George Salier Willis Nicholson served in two world wars, won the Military Cross, and was both an author and, during Prohibition, a rum-runner. Born in New Zealand, Nicholson lived for many years in Tofino and Victoria, and wrote Vancouver Island's West Coast, 1762-1962.

Nicholson was the unofficial mayor of Zeballos when the gold rush hit the Island community.

In the First World War, Nicholson served at Vimy before being injured at Arras. He was a major by the time the war ended. In the Second World War, Nicholson was a member of the Canadian Scottish regiment before being invalided home.

OLSON, Harold Benjamin (Barney)
Arena owner, died June 1, 1966

Harold Benjamin Olson was better known in Victoria as Barney Olson, the man who converted the Willows exhibition hall into a hockey rink. It burned down in April 1944, and Olson turned to other business ventures, including ownership of the Strathcona Hotel.

Olson had arrived in Victoria from the United States in 1912 with just $4 in his pocket. At times, he worked as a railway labourer, chauffeur and gasoline haulage contractor.

He started the rink after coming to Victoria to retire. His previous business interests had included bus lines and tour companies in the United States and throughout Western Canada as well as a miniature golf course and a roller rink.

PECK, Cyrus Wesley
Victoria Cross winner, died September 27, 1956

Cyrus Wesley Peck was the only person in the British Empire to win the Victoria Cross in the First World War while serving as a member of Parliament.

The Victoria Cross is the highest and most prestigious award for gallantry that can be awarded to British and Commonwealth forces.

When the First World War began he was in Prince Rupert working in a salmon cannery. He went overseas as a major in the 30th Battalion. In May 1915 Peck joined as a lieutenant colonel the 16th (Canadian Scottish) Battalion. He became commander of the regiment during the Battle of the Somme in 1916.

On September 2, 1918 at Cagnicourt, France, Peck's command, after capturing the first objective, was held up by enemy machine-gun fire. Peck made a personal reconnaissance under heavy fire, then reorganized his battalion and pushed forward.

He was elected to Parliament in 1917 as a Unionist for

• The ashes of James Nesbitt were placed at Ross Bay Cemetery.

the riding of Skeena. He was defeated in 1921. In 1924, he was elected as a Conservative MLA, and was re-elected in 1928.

A Gulf Islands ferry was named Cy Peck in his honour. Peck died in Resthaven Hospital in Sidney.

• A memorial to Cyrus Peck is in a cemetery in New Westminster.

PLASKETT, John Stanley
Observatory director, died October 17, 1941

John Stanley Plaskett was the recipient of more academic honours than any other Canadian of his day. He was instrumental in establishing the Dominion Astrophysical Observatory on Little Saanich Mountain in 1917, and served as its director for 18 years.

Plaskett published more than 100 papers on the optics of the telescope and spectroscope and other aspects of astronomy. He was a Fellow of the Royal Society of Canada, as well as a Fellow of the Royal Society of England, the highest scientific distinction in the British Empire.

PLAYFAIR, Alan
Military officer, died September 30, 1952

Alan Playfair served as a British army officer in India when the British monarch was the emperor of India. He was the son of Sir Robert Lambert Playfair, the British consul-general in Algiers, and was educated in England, Italy and Germany.

Playfair took part in the Sudan war in 1888-89, then went to India. He retired in 1921 and moved to Vancouver Island.

He bought the Sunset Inn in Qualicum Beach in 1927, and operated it for 10 years.

Playfair's son, Anthony Richard Playfair, was considered to be the first Canadian casualty of the Second World War. He was killed on September 9, 1939, when his airplane crashed in England because of enemy fire.

ROBINSON, Sir Heaton Forbes
Military officer, died July 13, 1946

Sir Heaton Forbes Robinson was born in Singapore in 1873. He was educated in London and worked on engineering projects in South Africa, South America and the Near East.

Sir Heaton attained the rank of lieutenant-colonel during the First World War, and was appointed deputy director of

works of the Imperial War Graves Commission in 1920. He became director in 1926 and held the position until 1938.

He retired to Victoria in 1939. While here he became known for his portraits, including ones of Sir Percy Lake, T.A. Rickard, and Eric Hamber, a former lieutenant-governor.

SCURRAH, Percy Beale
Victoria mayor, died July 14, 1970

Percy Beale Scurrah served as Victoria's mayor for six years.

He came to Victoria in 1909 and worked in insurance and real estate before opening a dress shop. He became interested in city hall in the late 1940s, and opted to run for council when he could not convince any of his friends to do so.

He was instrumental in the construction of a replacement for the Point Ellice Bridge, and worked to improve the city's financial situation.

SHACKLETON, Eleanor Hope
Pioneer nurse, died January 15, 1960

Eleanor Hope Shackleton worked as a nurse for half a century, in several countries and in war zones.

Her efforts were overshadowed by those of her brother, the famed Antarctic explorer Sir Ernest Shackleton.

SHANKS, Richard George (Bob)
Horse enthusiast, died November 7, 1991

Richard George Shanks – known as Bob from birth – ran a motorcycle shop, selling the Indian brand, before turning to saddlery instead. He took part in soccer, motorcycle riding and equestrian events, and bred thoroughbred horses.

In his spare time, Shanks wrote a book of verse.

His parents as well as his brother Reginald and sister Mollie are in Section I.

SHELFORD, Cyril Morley
Provincial politician, died November 8, 2001

Cyril Shelford served as agriculture minister for six years in the governments of W.A.C. Bennett and Bill Bennett.

Raised in the François Lake district of B.C., Shelford served in the Armed Forces and later worked as a logger and big game and fishing outfitter. Shelford only had a formal Grade 4 education and when he campaigned he wore his running shoes and drove around in a beat-up old truck.

In the late 1960s, Shelford took on the oil companies to fight for the equalization of gas prices throughout the province. As a result of his efforts, prices were lowered in northern B.C.

Shelford was elected in 1952 and was appointed to cabinet by the senior Bennett in 1968. He was defeated in 1972 but returned to the legislature in 1975, serving until 1979. He wrote four books, including From Snowshoes to Politics.

SIMONEAU, Leopold
Opera singer, died August 24, 2006

Leopold Simoneau was one of Canada's most acclaimed opera singers. He lived in Victoria for 20 years with his wife, soprano Pierrette Alaire.

The tenor rose to fame in the early 1940s singing with the Variétés lyriques, performing such well-known pieces as the Barber of Seville and La Traviata.

His career gained an international dimension in 1949 when he began performing in Paris, working with famed composer Igor Stravinsky among others.

Simoneau quickly developed a reputation as an expert interpreter of Mozart. He would go on to sing with many of the world's major orchestras, including New York's Metropolitan Opera and the Lyric Opera in Chicago.

In British Columbia the Simoneaus founded Canada Opera Piccola, an advanced training program for young singers. They were featured on a 51-cent stamp in 2006.

SINGH, Bala
First person cremated, died July 11, 1925

Bala Singh, who died in Nanaimo, was the first person cremated at Royal Oak. The cremation took place in a quarry that had been used to provide rocks for the cemetery's roads.

SPRATT, Marguerite Ethel
Shipbuilder, died July 31, 1946

Marguerite Ethel Spratt took over Victoria Machinery Depot when her husband Charles became ill. She ran the company for about 25 years, keeping it alive through the Depression years and then coping with the increase in shipbuilding orders that came with the Second World War.

Victoria Machinery Depot was one of the largest industrial companies on Vancouver Island.

When Spratt died, her will specified that her house could not be sold while her dog Rip was alive. Rip died three years after his master.

STEPHENSON, Emily Elizabeth
Island pioneer, died June 29, 1960

Emily Elizabeth Stephenson was the widow of a pioneer Anglican missionary among West Coast Indians. She was born in Metchosin in 1863, three weeks after her parents arrived from England. Her mother, Elizabeth Fisher, was the first school teacher in the area.

With her husband, Rev. Frederick Stephenson, Emily spent about 30 years among Indian bands in the Metlakatla and Port Simpson areas. She also lived in Ladysmith and Quamichan.

STEWART, Harry Alexander
Barber to the king, died November 7, 1956

Harry Alexander Stewart was a hairdresser in England, looking after clients such as King George V and Sir Winston Churchill.

He always said that he left England because he believed tariff rates should be reformed.

STIRLING, George Faulds
Provincial politician, died November 7, 1966

George Faulds Stirling was a CCF MLA for Salmon Arm. After serving in the legislature from 1943 to 1945, he remained in Victoria.

STOCKEN, Harry William Gibbon
Alberta missionary, died May 25, 1955

Rev. Canon Harry William Gibbon Stocken was a long-time missionary among the Blackfoot Indians of southern Alberta.

Born in England in 1858, Stocken arrived in Canada at

• The ashes of Marguerite Spratt were interred with her parents in Sacramento, California.

the age of 26 and immediately was sent to the Blackfoot reserve east of Calgary. He earned the name "Running Wolf." At the age of 63, he moved to Victoria to retire, but was named vicar of St. Martin's in the Fields.

He returned to visit the Blackfoot several times. His first flight in an airplane came when he was 90, with the fare paid by the Blackfoot.

TYRWHITT-DRAKE, Brian Halsey
Court official, died July 11, 1949

Brian Halsey Tyrwhitt-Drake was born into a pioneer family in 1866. He was called to the bar in 1890, appointed registrar of the Supreme Court in 1895, and was made registrar of the Exchequer Court in 1896. He was in charge of the bankruptcy office in Victoria.

He was also involved in many amateur theatre productions, and served as a major in the First World War.

VIRK, Reena
Murder victim, died November 14, 1997

Reena Virk was just 14 when she was brutally murdered under the Craigflower Bridge in 1997. She was swarmed by a group of teenagers, then dragged to the waters of the Gorge where she was drowned. The case drew international attention.

WISMER, Gordon Sylvester
Provincial politician, died December 28, 1968

Gordon Sylvester Wismer was attorney-general of British Columbia from 1937 to 1941 and from 1946 to 1952. He introduced many of the traffic regulations faced by B.C. drivers, and organized civil defence plans in the event that B.C. was bombed by the Japanese in the Second World War.

Wismer also tried to liberalize B.C.'s liquor laws, but failed to convince his cabinet colleagues. Before and after his political career, he worked as a criminal lawyer in Vancouver.

• The ashes of Sir Charles Seymour Wright were scattered over the side of HMCS Restigouche in Juan de Fuca Strait.

WRIGHT, Sir Charles Seymour
Scientist and explorer, died November 1, 1975

Sir Charles Seymour Wright was a member of the British Antarctic Expedition of 1910-1913 led by Robert Falcon Scott. Wright was the only Canadian among the six scientists on the expedition.

After Scott and the pole party went missing, Wright joined the search party of eight men and seven mules. In 1912 he discovered the tent where Scott had frozen to death.

After that, he lectured in England on cartography and surveying. In the First World War, he joined the Royal Engineers as a second lieutenant, and rose to the position of general staff officer in wireless intelligence.

During the Second World War, his work with the British admiralty included the development of naval radar, which gave British ships a decisive edge in the sea war. He was knighted by King George VI for his efforts.

He joined the staff at the Pacific Naval Laboratory at Esquimalt in 1955. In 1967, he joined the Institute of Earth Sciences at the University of British Columbia as well as Royal Roads Military College.

YOUNG, Henry Esson
Medical health officer, died October 24, 1939

Henry Esson Young was the provincial medical health officer for 23 years. Born in Quebec in 1867, Young worked as a doctor in Atlin, near the Yukon border, until he was elected to the provincial legislature in 1903.

As director of education, Young launched the tradition of free textbooks for school students in British Columbia.

He organized and had built a new provincial hospital for the mentally ill. It was known originally as Essondale, from Young's middle name. Today the site is known as Riverview, with a building named Henry Esson Young.

He is also remembered with the Young Building at Camosun College in Victoria.

Chinese memorials

In the newest areas of Royal Oak Burial Park, sections such as S, U and W, it would be hard not to notice that a high percentage of the markers bear Chinese characters. This is in sharp contrast to the oldest areas, where Chinese characters will not be found. Some markers bearing Chinese characters date from the 1940s, but they did not become commonplace until the early 1950s.

This is not a reflection of a demographic shift in Greater Victoria – after all, people born in China were some of the earliest permanent settlers here. Rather, the change resulted from the closure of the Chinese cemetery to new burials.

For half a century, until the early 1950s, Victoria's Chinese community had its own cemetery, owned by the Chinese Consolidated Benevolent Association, at Harling Point in Oak Bay. Before that cemetery was opened, the Chinese were forced to bury their dead in the least desirable areas of Ross Bay Cemetery. Land was acquired near Christmas Hill in Saanich, but opposition from local landowners made it impossible for the Chinese to use it as a cemetery. The CCBA bought the waterfront Oak Bay land as an alternative.

Initially, it appeared that the cemetery could be used indefinitely. Burial plots in the Chinese cemetery were not sold, but rather leased for six years. In the seventh year, the grave would be opened and the bones removed to be cleaned and dried and then returned to the person's home village in China.

This practice ended in 1937 because of the political situation in China. The original plan had been to reuse the plots, but with the shipments stopped, the cemetery quickly became full.

In 1961, the last 820 wooden crates of bones that had been awaiting shipment to China were buried in 13 mass graves at Harling Point. By that time, Royal Oak had already been the cemetery of choice in the Chinese community for almost a decade. The shift even extended into the past, with about 20 bodies from the Chinese cemetery exhumed and transferred to the burial park between 1958 and 1971.

Royal Oak had also recorded Chinese interments even when the Chinese cemetery was still in operation – and unlike Ross Bay, the Chinese at Royal Oak have always been buried in the same sections as everyone else.

Twice in the 1950s, the Chinese Consolidated Benevolent Association considered buying land adjacent to Royal Oak for a cemetery site. The property became part of Royal Oak Burial Park instead. The end result was the same, because many members of the Chinese community have been interred on the site selected by the CCBA a half-century earlier.

In the 1970s and 1980s, organizations in the Chinese community placed 11 group memorials in Royal Oak Burial Park. No remains are under the memorials, which simply serve as a tribute to the Chinese people who died in Greater Victoria over the years.

• One of the special plaques in memory of the Chinese pioneers in Victoria.

Society	Date	Section	Location co-ordinates	
Chinese Freemasons and Dart Coon Club	1977	Q	48°30.406	123°23.739
Chinese Nationalist League		R	48°30.586	123°23.803
Chinese Consolidated Benevolent Association	1984	Q	48°30.379	123°23.761
Hoy Sun Association		Q	48°30.380	123°23.763
Hook Sin Tong Charity Association	1987	M	48°30.505	123°23.814
Lim Say Hor Tong Society	1977	Q	48°30.403	123°23.733
Lung Kong Tin Yee Association	1985	Q	48°30.409	123°23.743
Shon Yee Benevolent Association	1977	Q	48°30.361	123°23.686
Wong Association	1984	Q	48°30.371	123°23.756
Yue Shan members	1985	Q	48°30.417	123°23.755
Yuen-Wo Society	1984	Q	48°30.424	123°23.760

Commonwealth War Graves

• Cross of Sacrifice

One of the most prominent features in the Royal Oak Burial Park is just inside the main entrance.

It is a Cross of Sacrifice, one of only 26 in North America, helping to mark the final resting places of those who lost their lives as a result of military action or training. The Cross of Sacrifice – a stone cross with a bronze sword – was placed in the burial park in 2004 by the Commonwealth War Graves Commission, which is responsible for the care of more than 1.7 million graves in 150 countries.

The location co-ordinates of the cross are N48°30.150 W123°23.058.

Royal Oak has 89 graves that are maintained by the war graves commission. They are in four different sections. The most visible of these graves are in Section D, which has 69 graves of airmen. Many of these men lost their lives while flying from Patricia Bay Airport doing air training or coastal patrols during the Second World War.

A flat memorial – noted in the list below as Coll. 3 – placed in 1944 has the names of flight officer Leslie Thomas Jordan, pilot officers Ewart Cecil Mitchell, Peter Dennison Metcalfe and Arthur Rockcliffe, and sergeants Bernard George Barker, Charles Peter Davidson, Lewis Philip Willetts, Andrew James Birrell, Frederick Laws, Leslie Mathias Langley and William Norman Jenkins. The men died in Sansum Narrows on October 4, 1944, on their last training flight. They would have graduated the next day.

An upright group memorial was placed at the edge of Section D in 2002. It pays tribute to eight Canadian airmen who died on August 23, 1942, when their Royal Canadian Air Force Stranraer flying boat went down in the ocean about 270 kilometres off Vancouver Island's west coast. The crew, flying out of Coal Harbour, had been on patrol after a reported sighting of a Japanese submarine. Another patrol plane later spotted the men in a dinghy, but rescuers never found any trace of them or their plane.

In addition to pilot Everard Cox, killed were: Sergeant Robert Bruce Stuart of Vancouver, Sergeant Kenneth E. Hope of Vancouver, Flight Sergeant Mervyn Cram of Renfrew, Ontario, Flight Sergeant Lawrence Alfred Bernard Horn of Regina, Sergeant A.W. Anderson of Selkirk, Manitoba, Sergeant C.F. Beeching of Regina, and Sergeant Leslie Oldford of Penhold, Alberta.

Graves of veterans who did not die as a direct result of military action or training are located throughout Royal Oak Burial Park. Look for large numbers of these graves in Section M, the south end of Section G and in D Extension.

A memorial granite bench dedicated to 394 men of the Canadian Scottish Regiment (Princess Mary's) who died during the Second World War is beside the entrance to the mausoleum.

Most of the 394 men were buried in Europe, close to where they fell.

The Commonwealth War Graves Commission markers at Royal Oak Burial Park:

Name	Location	Location co-ordinates	
Abbotts, Albert Henry	D-020-13	48°30.188	123°22.738
Adams, Robert William	D-011-05	48°30.180	123°22.775
Allan, John James	D-021-02	48°30.194	123°22.738
Bailey, William Benjamin Edward	D-021-19	48°30.190	123°22.734
Ball, Claude	B-09-06	48°30.230	123°22.990
Barker, Bernard George	D-019 Coll-03	48°30.184	123°22.739
Barrow, Richard Trathen	D-020-18	48°30.186	123°22.736
Bastick, Norman Arthur Albert	D-020-15	48°30.187	123°22.737
Beckley, Richard Lavern	B-08-24	48°30.226	123°22.991

Billingsley, Henry Kenneth	G-0162-G	48°30.262	123°22.953
Birch, Harold Charles	D-021-04	48°30.193	123°22.737
Birrell, Andrew James	D-019 Coll-03	48°30.184	123°22.739
Bishop, Colin Lisle	D-020-10	48°30.190	123°22.733
Bishop, Clarence Vivian	D-077-18	48°30.172	123°22.745
Bowler, Kenneth John	D-020-16	48°30.187	123°22.737
Bradley, Frederick George	D-020-11	48°30.188	123°22.738
Briggs, Jack Hanson	D-020-05	48°30.191	123°22.735
Brooks, Jerry Eaton	B-036-08	48°30.192	123°22.984
Brown, Ian McDonnell Sutherland	D-050-09	48°30.174	123°22.810
Caulkin, Thomas Henry	D-021-10	48°30.192	123°22.733
Christy, Richard Roland Thomas	D-021-09	48°30.192	123°22.733
Clarke, Theo Arden	D-083-14	48°30.153	123°22.776
Cliff, Albert Temple	B-076-27	48°30.171	123°23.017
Cockcroft, Robert Vernon	D-020-12	48°30.188	123°22.738
Coleman, Charles Francis	D-022-19	48°30.195	123°22.734
Cotton, Stanley Llewellyn	D-045-04	48°30.175	123°22.790
Cross, William Heber	D-047-17	48°30.172	123°22.802
Davidson, Charles Peter	D-019 Coll-03	48°30.184	123°22.739
Davis, Charles John	D-020-02	48°30.192	123°22.736
Dawson, Joseph	D-011-06	48°30.179	123°22.775
Deveson, Walter George	D-022-17	48°30.196	123°22.735
Dixon, Lorne Emerson	D-021-08	48°30.192	123°22.733
Dodson, John	B-078-02	48°30.167	123°23.023
Doherty, Andrew Joseph	D-020-17	48°30.187	123°22.736
Dyson, William John	D-021-15	48°30.191	123°22.735
Fear, Alec William Vernum	D-020-09	48°30.190	123°22.733
Fearnley, James French	D-021-13	48°30.192	123°22.736
Fenwick, William George	D-022-20	48°30.195	123°22.734
Fraser, James	B-08-28	48°30.224	123°22.992
Fraser, Lynn Pearson	D-021-17	48°30.191	123°22.735
Fraser, Rupert Brooke	D-022-12	48°30.196	123°22.735
Gaetz, Clifford James	A-018-10	48°30.207	123°23.016
Gimbert, George Alfred	D-020-20	48°30.186	123°22.735
Gould, Gordon Hugh	D-020-06	48°30.191	123°22.734
Gunn, John Cunningham	D-011-04	48°30.181	123°22.775
Hall, Charles Basil	D-E-H-027	48°30.106	123°22.764
Hayes, Roland	D-021-05	48°30.193	123°22.737
Hicks, Leonard Oscar	A-006-05	48°30.184	123°23.011
Houston, Allan Dale	D-021-01	48°30.194	123°22.738
Huard, Kenneth Charles	D-020-04	48°30.191	123°22.735

• The price of war: Richard Christy was just 19 years old when he was killed.

• Plaque near the Cross of Sacrifice provides information about the Commonwealth War Graves at Royal Oak.

• Some of Section D's Commonwealth War Graves Commission markers.

Hughes, Reginald John	D-020-03	48°30.192	123°22.736
Jenkins, William Norman	D-019 Coll-03	48°30.184	123°22.739
Jordan, Leslie Thomas	D-019 Coll-03	48°30.184	123°22.739
Kirchin, William	G-013-E	48°30.253	123°22.984
Langley, Leslie Mathias	D-019 Coll-03	48°30.184	123°22.739
Lawrie, James William	B-079-25	48°30.165	123°23.027
Laws, Frederick	D-019 Coll-03	48°30.184	123°22.739
Light, Maurice John	D-020-08	48°30.190	123°22.734
Lindgren, Stanley Henry	G-022-E	48°30.245	123°22.984
Linnell, George Victor	G-012-F	48°30.247	123°22.990
Maiden, Francis Keith	D-021-12	48°30.192	123°22.736
Marlow, Alan Robert	D-020-01	48°30.192	123°22.736
Martel, William Edward	G-022-D	48°30.246	123°22.983
Maynard, Roy Edward	D-022-10	48°30.198	123°22.734
Metcalfe, Peter Dennison	D-019 Coll-03	48°30.184	123°22.739
Mitchell, Ewart Cecil	D-019 Coll-03	48°30.184	123°22.739
McLeod, Herbert David	D-020-07	48°30.191	123°22.734
Newman, George Stanley Burt	D-021-03	48°30.194	123°22.738
Nicholls, Doris Ann	B-08-04	48°30.230	123°22.989
Oddy, Herbert Haste	G-013-F	48°30.252	123°22.984
Parson, James	B-010-15	48°30.228	123°22.999
Peterkin, James Smith	D-020-19	48°30.186	123°22.735
Pettit, Leslie	D-021-14	48°30.192	123°22.736
Richardson, Henry George McNaughton	B-07-30	48°30.223	123°22.986
Robertson, Thomas	D-E-I-031	48°30.103	123°22.766
Robson, James Thomas	D-022-18	48°30.196	123°22.735
Rockliffe, Arthur	D-019 Coll-03	48°30.184	123°22.739
Silcock, Herbert	D-050-20	48°30.174	123°22.812
Smith, Thomas	D-033-02	48°30.186	123°22.742
Smith, William James	B-08-05	48°30.229	123°22.988
Swetnam, Percy	B-017-19	48°30.208	123°22.977
Talbot, James Melville	D-021-06	48°30.193	123°22.737
Taylor, Selby Fred	D-021-16	48°30.191	123°22.735
Thomas, Norris	D-020-14	48°30.187	123°22.737
Thorne, John Oswald	D-021-20	48°30.190	123°22.734
Trudel, Paul Arthur	D-021-18	48°30.191	123°22.734
Wardlow, Tom Story	D-021-07	48°30.193	123°22.737
Weekes, Neville Oswald	D-021-11	48°30.192	123°22.736
Willetts, Lewis Phillip	D-019 Coll-03	48°30.184	123°22.739

• A view of the Triangle, taken from the road between Section A and Section B in the early 1940s.

For more information...

Many people want to know more about the people interred at Royal Oak Burial Park.

The burial park office can advise where a person is buried, as well as the date of burial. To do a search, the office staff will need the person's full name as well as an approximate date of death. Files rarely have more information than name, location and date of burial – and if they do, privacy regulations prevent the release of that information anyway.

The British Columbia Cemetery Finding Aid includes references to burials in Royal Oak Burial Park from 1923 to the middle of the 1970s. Information on the website includes the person's name and section where buried, but not the date or the complete reference to the location. The website is at www.islandnet.com/bccfa.

An index to deaths in British Columbia up to 20 years ago will be found on the website of the B.C. Archives, www.bcarchives.bc.ca. It provides the person's name, age, and location of death, as well as the death registration number, but does not include the name of the cemetery.

That information is available on the registrations themselves, available on microfilm at the Archives at 655 Belleville Street, Victoria. The registrations do not specify the location of a grave within a cemetery.

Newspaper obituaries often include references to the place of burial. In Greater Victoria, most obituaries appear in the Times Colonist, or, before September 1980, the Daily Colonist and the Victoria Times. Obituaries and death notices might also provide more information on the lives of the deceased, as well as the names of relatives. The old newspapers are on microfilm at the main branch of the Greater Victoria Public Library and at the McPherson library at the University of Victoria. Recent obituaries are on the Times Colonist website, www.timescolonist.com.

Information on the graves administered by the Commonwealth War Graves Commission can be found on the CWGC website, www.cwgc.org.

The staff members in the Royal Oak Burial Park office will help you determine the location of the marker you are looking for, based on the numbers and letters in the locator code. If you visit outside of office hours, you will be on your own.

The marker locations cited in this book include location references. If you have a Global Positioning System receiver, these references might help you determine the area where your person of interest is buried.

In most parts of the cemetery, it is simple enough to find a grave – just look for the small concrete squares that provide the section and plot information. In most of the sections – including H, I, J and K, and all those to the north of them – plots are numbered from south to north, and run in a zig-zag pattern. The pattern is also easy to follow in the southernmost sections. Section A is numbered from east to west, and sections B, C and the Triangle are numbered north to south.

In the older areas, D through G, you are most likely to need help from cemetery staff. The original three sections – E, F and G – were numbered from south to north in a zig-zag pattern, but there are many variations and inconsistencies. Many of the concrete locator markers are worn or missing. To make matters even worse, the northern part of F is known as F extension, because it was not part of the original development. The extension has its own numbering system.

Section D is numbered from north to south, but it wraps around a corner, crosses a road and includes a traffic circle. The numbering of D Extension is not related to the numbering in D, and it is the only area of the cemetery where plots are identified as being on the east or west sides of a road.

• This grave in Section E is easy to find, thanks to a raised plaque provided by the Saskatchewan government.

Discovering the burial park

Interested in exploring Royal Oak Burial Park? Here are some ideas for short walking tours.

1. Military. Start at the Cross of Remembrance, just inside the main gate. There is a map on a plaque near the cross that will help guide you to the areas with Commonwealth War Graves Commission markers. The best route is a circle route, visiting the markers in Section A, Section B and Section G, then on to the 69 markers in Section D before returning to the starting point.

2. Garden of Remembrance. The original section for cremated remains has been expanded twice. It is to the south of the crematorium, and offers an easy walk with many, many names of interest.

3. Leaders and pioneers. Start at the crematorium and head north in section C. You will see the grave of former Saskatchewan lieutenant-governor Thomas Miller, then the Patrick brothers of hockey fame. In Section D you can visit the markers for Bishop George Exton Lloyd and Charles Magrath, two noted Alberta pioneers. Then, go to Section E for Francis Rattenbury's first wife, former premier Simon Fraser Tolmie, the knighted Lake brothers and the first premier of Saskatchewan. Then head west to Section G to see the final resting place of "Honest" John Oliver, a former premier. Go north to Section H for suffragette and author Nellie McClung.

4. New developments. Start at the mausoleum, opened in 1996. Walk east, then south to the Memorial Woods and the Columbarium Grove. Go north to the new Woodlands natural burial section, then west to Section W, with its stone wall and raised markers. Finish by walking up the steps of the Terraces, past the section's fountain and water feature to the mausoleum.

5. Nature. At the northern edge of the D extension, look for a trail heading east into the trees. That trail will take you into the park that runs along the east side of Royal Oak Burial Park. You could walk to the top of the Boulderwood hill, or to the top of the burial park. Be warned that these trails are steep, and can be slippery when wet.

6. Perimeter. Royal Oak Burial Park has many regular visitors who see it as the perfect spot to get exercise and fresh air. A walk around the outside road measures 2.7 kilometres. Royal Oak has also been seen as a perfect spot for geocaching, the electronic treasure hunt. Several caches have been left in the park over the years.

• Section B – the first one seen on entry to Royal Oak Burial Park – has two distinctive rock walls. This photograph is from the 1940s.

Index to biographies

• Dave Obee is the author of Making the News: A Times Colonist Look at 150 Years of History as well as seven other books. He is the co-author, with Sherry Irvine, of Finding Your Canadian Ancestors: A Beginner's Guide.
Obee was born in British Columbia and has been a newspaper journalist for more than 35 years.